RAISING THE HARDY BOYS

"I love Nathalie Hardy's honest style and thoughtful portraits of family life. Hardy's quick, relatable essays are full of comfort, warmth, and humor. Raising the Hardy Boys is full of hope and everyday wisdom for anyone who's ever been part of a family."

Lela Davidson, author of Blacklisted from the PTA and Who Peed on my Yoga Mat? And, Managing Editor of ParentingSquad.com and Associate Editor of Peekaboo magazine.

"So it turns out parenting is hard. It's full of pitfalls and plot twists that mortals can't possibly fathom, much less prepare for. As humans with young offspring, we're usually satisfied with passing a day honoring the parent version of the Hippocratic oath--first do no harm. But then there's Nathalie Hardy. Not your mythical supermom, but a real person who keenly surveys these vexing moments that constitute parenthood. In her essays she indulges the best of our intentions and dissects our daily childrearing choices – the confounding, guilt-evoking and bliss-making scenes of our most meaningful experiences. In her overwhelming effort to shape small people, she shares the rarest of gifts – the courage of self examination."

Rob J. Dailey, author Goodbye Glamour Gals: a novel of women pilots in WWII and Chehalem Cultural Center Executive Director

"With warmth, humor, and humility, Nathalie Hardy writes about not only the development of her child, but her development as a parent."

Janice Erlbaum, author of Girlbomb: A Halfway Homeless Memoir and Have You Found Her: A Memoir

"One of the toughest parts of being a parent is that you sometimes feel alone, like there is no way anyone can relate to what you are going through. *Raising the Hardy Boys* will not only reassure you that you are very much part of a universal experience, it will remind you to look for the humor and joy in the trying times of parenthood."

Bianca Kajlich, actress (Undateable, Rules of Engagement) and co-host of Atomic Moms

"I'm a mother of four boys. When I read one of Nathalie's columns I feel like I've just talked to my sister, and I feel like I want to call her right back, because I've remembered one more thing she just has to hear. Nathalie is like that – really comfortable and totally real – she writes everyday, honest, comic relief, with zero pretense and I just really like that."

Stacy Julian, Founder of Big Picture Classes and author of The Big Picture (Scrapbooking Your Life and More) and Photo Freedom and Founding Editor of Simple Scrapbooks magazine

"When Nathalie Hardy approached me about launching a new-mother advice column in the *News-Register*, we mutually resolved it would substitute real-life, common-woman, on-the-job experience for expert advice and professional jargon. It would be bright, sassy and down to earth. It would talk straight across, woman-to-woman, not downhill, expert-to-novice. She succeeded wonderfully with it — so wonderfully that she was persuaded to offer a selection of her work in book form.

"Please plunge in. You will find yourself laughing, crying and commiserating with a kindred spirit."

Steve Bagwell, Managing Editor Yamhill Valley News-Register

Awards . . .

2014 and 2013 Oregon Newspaper Publishers Association's Better Newspaper Contest, First place for Best Local Column.

2013 National Newspaper Association Better Newspaper Contest, Third place for Best Serious Column. Judges noted: "Hardy writes with grace about the universal search for identity, the never-ending quest to understand that we are exactly what we were meant to be."

2013, 2012 and 2010 Oregon Society of Professional Journalists Excellence in Journalism Column, First place for Best Column.

2012 National Newspaper Association Better Newspaper Contest, Third place for Best Humorous Column. Judges noted: "all parents can relate."

2010 National Newspaper Association, Third place for Best Humorous Column.

2009 National Newspaper Association, Second place for Best Humorous Column. Judges noted: "cute, all too true."

RAISING THE HARDY BOYS*

They said there would be bon-
bons

BY NATHALIE HARDY

A collection of nationally award-winning columns
written in the margins of motherhood.

*Not to be confused with a how-to book.

Ridenbaugh Press
Carlton, OR

Copyright © 2014 Nathalie Hardy
Ridenbaugh Press
P.O. 834, Carlton OR 97111
(503) 852-0010
www.ridenbaughpress.com
stapilus@ridenbaugh.com
All Rights Reserved.
No part of this book may be reproduced, stored in a retrieval system, or
transmitted in any form by any means, without prior permission of the publisher.

Composition and editing by Ridenbaugh Press, Carlton, Oregon.
Cover design and art work by Scott Carl.
Author photo by Carrie Hardy.
Columns in this book were previously published.

Library of Congress Cataloging-in-Publication Data:
Hardy, Nathalie
Raising the Hardy Boys: They Said There Would Be Bon-Bons
ISBN 978-0-945648-25-3 (softbound)
1. Columns-Parenting. 2. Memoir. I. Title.
Printed in the United States of America.
December 2014
10 9 8 7 6 5 4 3 2 1

Contents

2011

2014

Dedication

This book is dedicated to Samuel Knox and Jacob Henry without whom there would be no Hardy Boys for me to raise. There aren't enough words to express how thankful I am to be their mom, specifically, and that I get to be a mom at all.

I love these two to the moon and back. Unless they are mad at me in which case, in Sam's words, it's "to the planet before Pluto and back."

Or, in Jake's words: Even when their "hearts are dark at me."

It is my greatest joy to see them grow into themselves.

Sam and Jake, I'm taking good notes because childhood doesn't keep.

Let's savor them later.

And also, to Matt who said "I do" and "you can." And, for always believing in my writing. And for understanding that deadlines come before dusting. But also, so do most things. The boys are blessed to call you "Daddy."

Also, this is for the mamas. And the dads. However they came to fill those roles.

And for those who love them.

Introduction

Whenever it comes up that I write a parenting column, I'm quick to clarify it is in no way a "how to" guide.

Though I suppose I do sometimes offer guidance in the way of: "do not try this at home."

Read at your own risk, is all I'm saying.

So, now that we've established what this book is not, I'd like to tell you what it is. I really would. Except I don't know, not exactly.

Every year when it's time to submit entries for newspaper competitions I look over my collection and wonder how to answer that.

Essentially, I write in the margins of motherhood—and everything else—then I work these notes into a monthly column about what it's like raising my two young boys. Are my columns funny? Are they serious? They don't fit into any one box neatly. Yeah, I know: that is totally a metaphor for my life. Or is that not what you were thinking? Moving on, then.

I've won awards for "best humorous column" though I actually write about subjects as light as bulimia, bullying, birthing plans and breastfeeding. But also bon-bons. And barf, and birthdays.

It seems this book is brought to you by the letter 'b.' There's also a brief mention of Barbados (Nope, not a Travel to the Tropics with Tots story. That's just what I called the birthing room at the hospital).

Then again, despite fantasizing about umbrellas in my drinks, I've won in the "serious column" category as well. Probably all the stuff about self-esteem erosion, suicide, school shootings and shame. Just guessing. (And thank you letter 's'.)

You guys want to know how I celebrated my first national award for my column? I calmly hung up with my editor. Then I squealed, which startled the baby. Then I went back to stuffing the inserts into diapers.

My own take on the Zen proverb, "After enlightenment, the laundry."

The columns in this collection are primarily in the same form as they ran in the paper, with a few minor edits. It was a struggle to hit my 600-word-count limit with some of these topics. My editors might even be surprised to learn I know what the word count is supposed to be.

It has come to my attention recently that not everyone leans into awkward, messy, possibly painful things like, say, feelings, be they our own or those of others.

Then, there are people like me who can feel what others are feeling, sometimes even before they do. I know, awkward, right? It's okay, you don't have to talk about your feelings or anything, but I will. Mine, not yours. Unless you can relate. And if so, you can just nod silently. Or email me or something. Either way, you can know you're understood. And sometimes, a lot of the time, that's enough.

I've been keeping it real since before that was even a thing. In my journals, anyway. For more than half of my life I was excruciatingly shy and a host of other unfortunate adjectives.

But now everything is all better. Except not. But I've learned that inner peace thing people talk about is only possible when you give in to fully embracing your life exactly as it is instead of lamenting the one you thought you would, or should, have.

I've always processed my life through writing in real time. Now, I share parts of it in my columns, and with you, because I know how much it helped me see myself, my experiences and the darkest parts of my heart reflected in the words of others. I believe in the power of telling—and owning—our stories.

I also write a tiny bit about wanting to put my head in the oven. Not, however, because I think there is anything funny about suicide, but because depression is real and I use humor—albeit inappropriate at times—to cope. You're welcome.

When I imagined what motherhood would be like, I was missing a few things, including a kid and a crystal ball.

Let's just say, I realized quickly things weren't going to look like the picture. I think parenting and life are less about having all the answers and more about learning now to react to being thrown off. I think it's about learning how to find your balance when the ground below you has become unsteady, and I often lose my balance between being the mom I want to be and the me I used to be.

So I suppose the answer to what this book is all about might be that it's a collection of my notes as I've found my voice as a mother, and a writer, during the course of staying home with a baby, having another baby, going to work fulltime in a newsroom and then coming back home, waiting for Oprah to call.

You might be wondering if I'm planning to mention my boys at all, being as how this is supposed to be a book about them. That's the thing, though. It's not actually about them. It's about my experience as a mother. It's a fine line, but one I am very mindful of when it comes to what I publish.

Initially my column ran as "Baby on Board" and started running in the *Yamhill Valley News-Register* in McMinnville, Oregon. The column launched in May of 2008. Sam was seven months old and had just started eating solid foods. At this writing, he is seven years old.

And somewhere in between, roughly when I was getting the hang of things, we welcomed Jake into our family in January of 2010. And with Jake, "Raising the Hardy Boys" was born. Later, I started writing two more columns for special sections "Confessions of a Green Wannabe" and "Behind the Picket Fence", a few of which I've included in this collection.

With every column I've written, I've asked myself if I was putting something out into the world that would mortify them in a locker room someday. Of course, I expect they'll be able to take a joke or two 'cause we're raising resilient kids here, but still...

So this book, and my columns, have always and intentionally been about me and my experiences as their mother. That is my story to tell. The rest belong to them.

Funny story though, when my boys found out my columns were going to be published into a book, there was an awkward silence.

It turns out, my now seven and four-and-three-quarter-year-old boys don't want to be in a book. Because, they said, "people might laugh at us."

"Here's the thing," I told them, "you can't make decisions based on what other people might do." I also told them nothing will protect them from being laughed at. It's what you do about it that counts. It's what you think about people laughing at you that matters. And we are in control of what we think. I don't expect them to master that concept immediately, some of us take a lifetime to get that, but it seemed worth mentioning.

Before moving forward I needed to make sure they really weren't upset about the idea of this book. I'm a writer, after all, I can only afford so much therapy.

I did not point out that at least I'm not writing about doing smack on the bathroom floor. I'll save that stuff for another book. Not that I've done heroin on the bathroom floor. Or ever, anywhere.

But there are stories for another time, maybe.

Anyhow, after we talked through it, Sam said: "Fine. But just so you know, I'm going to write one about you when I grow up."

Well-played, Sam. I kept that threat/promise in mind during the final edits.

The threads of my story will get tangled in theirs, and we'll have to sort all that out. Hopefully you'll find something in these pages that resonates or reminds you of something cherished. Either way, I hope you take a few notes in the margins.

P.S. If you're just here about the bon-bons—spoiler alert: I'm sorry no one told you, but that's a joke. That's not a thing.

I know! Secretly, I'm still looking, too.

A baby is born—and a column

MAY 6

Before I became a mom, I had lots of reasons why I wasn't ready. Long lists of them.

For one thing, I still didn't fold my own clothes. For another, I didn't know nearly enough about nutrition.

The food pyramid? Are you kidding me?

Then there was the fact that I didn't know all my state capitals, or my multiplication table past the 10s. I didn't know any lullabies and couldn't seem to fully swear off swearing.

Besides, I figured I needed a minimum of eight hours of sleep to behave remotely human. And, I'm definitely not a morning person.

Then, on October 7, this 8-pound, 8-ounce bundle of awesome came into my world, and none of that mattered any more.

I do, however, find myself wondering why it is that I have manuals for everything from our washing machine to our weed whacker, but when it comes to the care and feeding of a newborn, all I've got is Google.

During our first week together, I was stunned at how little Sam could do for himself. I wasn't expecting him to make his own bed or anything, but frankly, his neediness was a little overwhelming.

Luckily, as my list of things to worry about grew exponentially longer the moment Sam was born, so did my belief in my ability to take care of him one way or the other. Never in my life have I been so self-conscious and self-confident at the same time.

I figured I couldn't be the only one feeling such see-saw emotions. And since I'm already in the habit of taking notes on everything, I figured I'd combine that with my background in journalism and out of that something else was born: the idea for a monthly column in which I delivered the scoop from the baby beat.

I earned my degree at Western Washington University in Bellingham. Along the way, I did a reporting internship at the [McMinnville, OR] *News-Register*.

I later worked professionally for a paper on the Oregon Coast. And I've done a lot of freelancing.

I write like I live—in full-disclosure mode. And I do it on purpose.

I've been "keeping it real" since before that was a thing.

I think that if all of us go around acting like everything is OK, keeping all of our angst to ourselves, it makes us feel there must be something wrong with our internal wiring.

Everyone else seems to be coping. Why not me? What's wrong with me?

Sam was seven weeks old before it occurred to me that we were going to be fine. Better than fine, even. I looked Sam in the eye and I told him I wasn't afraid of him any more.

Up to that moment, I'd entertained occasional fantasies of leaving the baby monitor turned up full blast on my husband's side of the bed with a note stuck to the antenna. But even in my fantasies, I realized I could never follow through.

Would I ever leave my family? No. No, I wouldn't.

That doesn't mean I don't occasionally long for moments all to myself, though, without my Baby Barnacle.

I'd love the time to take a leisurely shower, maybe even do something with my hair. My current beauty regime consists of lip gloss, a rubber band and a wet washcloth to dab at stains.

When I first had Sam, I braced myself for public criticism and judgment. Instead, I've been delighted by helpful, friendly and supportive people.

Well, mostly. The occasional public criticism we'll save for another day.

Parenting can be such a divisive issue. Yet it seems to me we're all driven by a desire to do our best by our children.

My intention with this column is to tell the truth about being a new parent, with no apologies.

I'm no Kelly Ripa—but so what?

JUN 3

People like to tell new parents, "Enjoy every minute of it!"

It's such an innocent, well-meaning statement. Yet it makes me cringe.

Really? Every minute? Who does that?

Make no mistake. I am grateful for the opportunity to be a mom. However, I have enough to feel guilty about without worrying that I am not enjoying every single moment that is the bliss of being a new— sleep-deprived, delirious, confused and over-Googled—mom.

I had a very un-enjoyable meltdown recently. And I blame Kelly Ripa.

In case you've missed her commercial, encouraging moms to be "even more amazing," it goes like this: Ripa glides her size-perfect, post-partum self from her glamorous job to the store, and then on to her immaculate home, without breaking a bead of sweat or mussing a single hair. There, she proceeds to simultaneously host a dinner party for adults and sleepover for kids.

The roast is perfect, the mac-n-cheese just right. The juice boxes are chilled to the perfect temperature. There are no bits of avocado in her hair, no spit-up on her pants and no Cheerios on the floor.

On top of all that—and this is what kills me—she seems to be enjoying every second of it. Come. On.

As a result of my Kelly Ripa Reckoning, I've decided to focus on what I think makes a good mother, based on my values, and then say "yes" to myself more often, instead of saying yes to someone else. I had gotten off track trying to be the mom others felt I should be.

Before Sam was born, I was worrying about just that sort of thing. My husband assured me: "You'll be exactly the mom our baby needs."

Take that Kelly Ripa! Whenever I start getting worked up over details, I cite my new mantra: Forget perfect and amazing. Embrace good enough.

My new "personal values" approach created some fun opportunities for us this month as we ventured out to try new things. Sam and I checked out a couple of new parks, enjoyed story time at Third Street Books and attended a baby-wearing class at the library.

Baby-wearing? Yep. It features a fabric sling, the hands-free way to cuddle your little one.

When I spotted the class listed in the *News-Register*'s Events Calendar, I flashed back to when Matt and I opened a shower gift called a "Moby Wrap," only to find miles of cloth unraveling.

We took one look at each other, stuffed it back into the pouch and shook our heads. No way. Too confusing.

For starters, I can't tie a knot. Seriously. Sam will have to wear flip-flops and Velcro-closers until a teacher takes pity on him and teaches him what his Mama can't.

Besides the no-strings simplicity attraction, there was the Earth Mama attraction. Carrying Sam in his sling seemed just so, well, right.

I was afraid I would feel like a total misfit at the library session, but I went with a friend and her girls anyway. And we all loved it.

The presenters were helpful. They brought a variety of slings and wraps for us to try out, as well as enough patience to teach us how to put them to use.

I was so in love with my sling afterward, that I walked around town feeling so very Earth Mama proud. Sam snuggled in so quickly, he was napping by the time we got back to the car.

In addition to learning something new, spending a wonderful afternoon with a friend and meeting new moms in the area, I got the gift of a hands-free way to cuddle my baby! If you're curious, check out Valley Sling Babes at www.nwbabywearers.org.

Try something new of your own this month. Then let me know how it goes.

Meanwhile, if you get tempted to play the comparison game, remember this: As long as we rank somewhere between Britney Spears and Kelly Ripa, we're doing good enough.

Skyping across the continents

JUL 1

When my husband and I moved to Oregon, we didn't realize that we would someday miss having family nearby.

That someday came when Sam was born and our parents became his proud grandparents. Suddenly being on our own wasn't so great.

My mother and mother-in-law took turns helping us when Sam first came home.

I cried when we dropped my mom off at the airport. I also cried when my mother-in-law pulled out of the driveway to head back to Walla Walla. But I wasn't just crying for myself.

My parents used to tell me they wanted things for us that they didn't have. Now I understand.

Since my relationship with my grandparents was defined by the absence of one, I want better for Sam. But with one set of grandparents living in Europe and the other living a day's drive away, how do we accomplish that?

People say you can't put a price on freedom, but when my parents escaped communist Czechoslovakia in 1970, the cost was high. In exchange for freedom, they had to leave everything and everyone behind.

Of course, I am thankful they sacrificed so much to raise us in a free country. But every now and then, like on Grandparents Day at school, I felt I was missing out on something special.

My grandparents loved me, but it was from so very far away. And this was before the days of e-mail and cheap international calling plans.

Flash forward to the fall of communism and the proliferation of the Internet instead of nuclear weaponry. That induced my parents to move back to Slovakia.

But they still manage to be with Sam for breakfast most days of the week. Golf games scheduled to beat the afternoon heat in their hometown of Piestany are more of a problem than the 5,500 miles and nine-hour time difference separating us.

So how are my parents managing to stay connected to the little boy who made them the grandparents they waited so long and impatiently to become?

It's called Skype, a software program that allows us to make free video-enhanced phone calls over the Internet. And it works equally well calling my parents in another continent as it does calling Matt's parents in another state.

As a person who still hasn't figured out how to send pictures from her phone, I was a little reluctant to try Skyping. I was hooked, though, once I saw the delight on my parents' faces as they got to know Sam on camera before they ever got the chance to meet him in person.

Sam starts flapping his arms, flinging Oatios and grinning as his grandparents come into focus. During our cross-continental breakfasts, my parents and I chat while I attempt to get Sam to take another bite.

From across the world, my mom coaxes Sam to open his mouth by making funny faces and noises. As I watch her, I get a flashback to my time on the other side of the high chair.

I treasure these casual conversations. I also treasure the technology that allows my parents to be there for something as ordinary as watching Sam discover apricots.

The flashbacks aren't mine alone either.

One afternoon, after Sam had thrown a day-long fit about I'm not sure what, I was exasperated. I told my mom I was amazed at how stubborn he could be.

She watched Sam give me this little look, mid-tantrum, and simply said, "Oh." It turns out she recognized that look from 32 years ago.

Ideally, our parents would be here to love Sam in person. But when circumstances create the need for long-distance grandparenting, it's nice to know that with the help of good intentions and good technology, we can maintain a strong connection between Sam and his grandparents.

Finding Giraffe and losing my marbles

AUG 5

From the moment I met him, I was crazy in love with my son—the kind of crazy that would make me do ridiculous, embarrassing things in pursuit of his sweet smile.

My most recent display of maternal madness invited endless mocking. And I don't even care.

Let me start at the beginning.

When he was 4 months old, Sam picked the stuffed animal that would become The One. He just plucked it out of his crib one morning and never let go—except to bathe.

Since then, he's kept Giraffe faithfully by his side every waking minute—at least every waking dry minute. More importantly, Giraffe plays an integral part in Sam's very specific and somewhat obsessive bedtime routine.

Giraffe is so well-loved—read disgustingly dingy—that several people suggested we buy another one just in case. And I added that to the list of things I should probably do—right after I order a birth certificate and hospital pictures.

I kind of forgot about it until Giraffe mysteriously disappeared. And at bedtime, no less!

At first, I blamed Lucy, our Labrador puppy. I searched all of her hiding spots, finding two unmatched socks, a teething toy and the wrapper from a cube of butter, but no Giraffe.

While Matt went through Sam's bedtime routine: bath, two books, three drops of lavender, baby massage with the Burt's Lotion I tore the house and car apart.

Finally, I took a drive, retracing the steps of our afternoon walk. I ended up searching the park.

"Hi, Mrs. Hardy!" a chorus called from the pool.

I froze. For the first time, it occurred to me that it wasn't bedtime for anyone else in Carlton, and I was out in public in my pajama bottoms and nursing top, frantically searching for a stuffed animal.

Sam eventually managed to fall asleep without Giraffe, but I didn't. I tossed and turned all night wondering what had happened to it.

As I'd searched for Giraffe around town, I'd noticed missing animal fliers posted on public bulletin boards. And a light went on.

So what if it's not a real animal, I figured, as I posted missing fliers of my own for Sam's beloved Giraffe. In retrospect, it did look like an ad for a missing child, what with a picture of Sam and Giraffe accompanied in big, bold type the words, "Have you seen me?"

OK, a flier might have been a little dramatic, maybe even a little misleading.

When my husband asked me to e-mail him a copy at work, I was touched. That is, I was until I learned he had forwarded my e-mail around the office with this message: "My son lost his stuffed animal. My wife lost her mind."

Mock me if you must, but it worked. Yep, that's right.

Sam was reunited with Giraffe the next afternoon. It seems Giraffe had fallen out of Sam's stroller near city hall, and I got several phone calls alerting me to the fact.

Some people—and you know who you are—suggested the missing giraffe was more a problem for me than Sam.

There might be a little bit of truth to that, but I have to tell you, when Sam was reunited with Giraffe, his face lit up like I'd never seen before. He stroked Giraffe's ear and gazed adoringly at him all the way home. He clung to Giraffe the rest of the afternoon.

As I watched the look of relief and joy spread across his face, I knew I was committed to being as crazy as it takes to keep that smile on his face.

Their baby's famous, ours came first

SEP 2

"Oh, no she didn't!"

I kept repeating it as I found myself wading in the shallow end of pop culture again, livid at the birth announcement for the world's most famous twins.

"Why is this even news?" I muttered to no one in particular.

First, Angelina Jolie steals my boyfriend. Then, she has the nerve to give their love child the same name I so carefully chose for my son, thereby changing the conversation he will have about it for the rest of his life.

Second only to becoming parents, what to name our baby is the biggest decision my husband and I have made. It was no easy feat, as both of us worked in public schools, where we were exposed to the best and worst associations with many names.

Then, there was the fact that we each had some baggage with our own names.

Matt's parents, who swear they never hit the peace pipe or go on gambling binges, gave all three of their children names with 21 letters.

For Matt, this meant dropping one of the 't's commonly used in Matthew. It also meant spending most of his school years as 'Matt H.'

Then there was me.

As a painfully shy kid, I dreaded roll on the first day of school. The teacher would call out, "Anna," then pause while she struggled with the rest of my name. "Naythalee Orvateez?"

"It's Oravetz," I'd explain. "And the 'Anna' and the 'h' in Nathalie are silent."

I'd cringe at the snickers behind me as the teacher corrected her roster.

We thought we'd spared Sam all of that first-day-of-school awkwardness when we finally settled on "Samuel Knox." His first name is a classic and his middle name is unique, in addition to being meaningful to us. And yeah, the "K" is silent.

Our son's name contains our hopes for the person he will become: confident, easy-going, creative and true to himself. We figured he'd pick which one he wanted to use as he made his way through life.

We got a lot of flak from both sides of the family about our selection, but we paid little mind and filled out his birth certificate as planned.

Then, a few months later, it happened. My son's unique name was hijacked by Angelina Jolie and thrust into the spotlight of public opinion.

I was devastated when Brad and Angelina named their son "Knox." What started as a meaningful name for us for our first born would forever elicit this response: "Knox? Like Brangelina's kid?"

Lest you think I exaggerate the potential ramifications of this disaster, I assure you Brad and Angelina have serious pull with name rankings. According to the Social Security Administration's website, Maddox and Shiloh—the names of two of Jolie-Pitt's children—are steadily climbing in popularity. If Sam decides to go by his middle name, he may end up being a "Knox H." OK, probably not. But still.

Flash forward to Sam's first day of school. His teacher will raise her eyebrows and try not to roll her eyes as she pegs us as celebrity fanatics.

I will, of course, teach Sam to say, "I was born first." But it will be too late. Assumptions will be made.

To find out the top baby names visit www.socialsecurity.gov. The site features a list of the 1,000 most popular names for each year since 1880.

For the record, 'Knox' hasn't made the top 1,000 since 1888.

I hope Sam likes his name. I really do.

But whether my son thinks his name is good, bad or indifferent, I hope he grows up to be the kind of guy who knows that the names we are given are far less important than the one we make for ourselves.

Baby brings a year of surprises

OCT 7

I know a character played by Chevy Chase in the 1985 movie, "Spies Like Us," isn't a likely source for parenting advice. But Chase's classic line, "We mock what we don't understand," has become my mantra as a new mom.

Since the day Sam was born, I've been eating a steady dose of humble pie.

I was one of those people who thought having a kid wouldn't change my life all that much. Sure, we'd get a car seat and follow some basic safety measures. But overall, I figured we'd still do our thing and the baby would adapt.

As things turned out, we've been doing the majority of the adjusting. We're home by 5:30 every evening and planning our life around his sleep schedule.

Before Sam was born, I had this lovely vision of him playing and sleeping ever so sweetly beside me as I worked. In reality, I wear him on my back while balancing my laptop in front of a mirror so he can play with his "friend" while I work in short bursts.

Karmic justice really socks it to me when I take Sam out in public. I cringe as I strap Sam into his plush grocery cart cover, because I recognize the looks we get.

I used to make the same face at what I considered excessive baby gear. I really had no clue how indiscriminate kids were in tasting life.

Sam's governing creed seems to be, "Hmm. That looks interesting. I think I'll give it a little lick."

If he can't lift it, no problem. He'll bring his tongue down to the item of interest, be it a shoe, a door hinge or the handle of a stranger's grocery cart.

I love him, but that's kind of disgusting.

Time is another concept that's changed for me since Sam was born. As in, where did it go? The first year of Sam's life has gone by in as much of a blur as his image in his ultrasound pictures, which I still haven't scrapbooked.

Until recently, I wondered why my mom never finished my baby book. During college, she gave me the pink album with my name and birth weight filled out and an envelope of my first lock of hair tucked inside.

I get it now, Mom.

This column publishes on Sam's first birthday and, I must confess, his scrapbook isn't finished. In truth, it isn't even started. Sam will most likely go off to college with a box I lovingly pack for him and label, "Stuff I meant to scrapbook." It'll be full of memorabilia, camera memory cards and a coupon for Costco.

I also used to wonder how people could talk so much about their kids. Look at me now, sharing the inside scoop on mine with you and enjoying hearing about your parenting experiences and memories, as well as what you'd like to see in future columns.

Am I surprised at how such a small person could turn my life completely upside down? Sure. But as I look at my blonde-haired, blue-eyed boy with his impish smile and contagious laugh I am even more surprised that while I've only known him 12 months, I can't begin to remember what life was like before he arrived.

As I celebrate his first birthday with my husband, we tip our party hats to honor our son's first year of life and all the ways he's grown and changed since the day he joined us on the planet. But I also have to give a little nod to the way we, his parents, have changed and grown since our little 8 pound, 8 ounce bundle of awesome came into our world.

Political wars, meet parenting wars

NOV 11

For what feels like forever, our country has gone about business as usual during a general election, discussing key issues—wardrobes and lipstick, be it on a pig or a pit bull, along with the usual campaign trail gimmicks.

While all this has finally come to an end as you read this column, another kind of politics, the politics of parenting, will continue to play out across the nation—in playgrounds, parks and PTA meetings—regardless of who is running the country.

I don't know if it's always been this way, but modern day parenting boils down to making a lot of decisions: Cloth or disposable? Vaccinate or withhold? Bottle or breast, and for how long?

However you answer those questions, you end up making some kind of statement. You end up contributing to debates in our living rooms, chat rooms and grocery store checkout lines.

Yes, grocery store lines. Recently, a new mother and I got to chatting, as we new mothers tend to do, while buying healthy snacks for our bambinos. Within seconds, the subject turned to sleeping, a near guarantee in these introductory new mom chats.

We sheepishly confessed to one another that no, our little ones were not sleeping through the night yet.

I went first, and admitted we'd finally taken the doctor's advice and tried letting him "cry it out." It felt awful, but it's helping, I reported.[*]

I saw joy and understanding in her eyes as she shared her similar findings. Both the joy and understanding evaporated, though, as the person scanning our groceries told us how heartless it was of us to do that to our babies.

"What kind of mother just lets her baby cry?" she demanded. "That's just awful!" she scolded.

Nice.

As we skulked out of the store, the other heartless mother and I simply wished each other good luck.

---

[*] Through the lens of retrospect it didn't actually work for us and I wouldn't put myself, or Sam, through that experience again but I was judging myself enough and desperate for sleep. I didn't need the random disapproval of a well-rested stranger. Nobody does.

Sleep theories aside, perhaps no issue is more emotionally loaded than the one about moms who work outside the home versus those who stay home with their children. As one reader who's had it both ways put it: "It's much easier to be considered lazy because you choose to stay home than be considered heartless because your child's in day care and being 'raised by someone else.' What really is the point of mothers passing judgment over other mothers?"

The moment I read her painful words, I committed to feeling less self-conscious and apologetic about my new stay-at-home mom status.[*]

Why was I apologetic?

I felt there was a stigma to being a stay-at-home mom, but I couldn't quite describe how I felt about it until the other day as I was cleaning. It's something I'm starting to do more as a safety thing for Sam than out of any natural domestic inclination. I realized I was holding a jar of Murphy Oil and two magazines—Good Housekeeping and Ms. At that moment, my inner turmoil came into focus.

Who am I now, exactly? I wondered what my old activist self would think of the me of today—the one swapping recipes and child care tips between playing peek-a-boo, reading "Click, Clack, Moo" and changing diapers endlessly.

It hit me that I'm still the same person, even though what I do during the day has changed. The measure of my success no longer comes in the form of paycheck, but in the form of a mostly clean house, more frequent healthy homemade food and a healthy, happy little handful I'm proud to call my son.

Now that the question of who will be our new president is resolved, I have some new ones:

How long will it be before these so-called "mommy wars" end? Has parenting always been so political?

What were your parenting land mines? And, perhaps most importantly, where are the bon-bons?

---

[*]   Now that I've had it both ways, I can say the pitting mama's against each other is madness. It's just a different kind of hard, and awesome, either way. Perhaps the most difficult part is dealing with assumptions people make by projecting their own stuff. Eyes on your own paper, people!

The joys of being a holiday mom

DEC 2

If you're into decking the halls for the holidays, knock yourself out. But, if what you actually feel like decking is the next person who mentions how many shopping days are left until Christmas, this one's for you.

I knew I wanted to be a holiday mom long before Sam was born.

I imagined decorating my home with twinkling lights, putting up a fancy tree, wrapping beautiful gifts, baking luscious cookies, sending out personalized Christmas cards featuring photos of family members in matching sweaters, maybe even going out caroling.

Oh, yeah. And all of this would be done calmly and kindly.

Flash forward to reality.

My first chance at being a holiday mom last year found me not so much calm and not at all kind. I lost myself in the holiday hoopla and forgot why I loved the holidays in the first place—the connections celebrated with family, neighbors, friends and strangers.

The whole point of being a holiday mom was to make the holidays special, not stressful. Here I was trying to make Sam's first Christmas perfect, and I was too stressed out to see it was just another day to him.

Just another day to be loved and cuddled. Just another day to celebrate being part of a warm family. That and some boxes with ribbon on them.

With advertisements for gift ideas appearing prominently ever since Halloween, it's easy to feel "behind" before the calendar even turns to December. So what's it take to avoid experiencing a merry little meltdown?

Two things. Focus on your values and practice this one word sentence: No.

According to the American Psychological Association, financial concerns are the leading cause of holiday stress. It's helpful, especially in leaner times, to remember that the real spirit of Christmas has nothing to do with what's in the box and everything to do with what's in the heart.

Since there are only 22 days left till Christmas—sorry about that—

I'm not advocating you start crafting a slew of handmade gifts for the big day.

That is, not unless you already started on that months ago. If that's the case, bully for you.

For the rest of us, I suggest shopping locally and creatively.

Consider gifts that give back year-round, like a photo calendar or magazine subscription. How about buying a fun trinket at a favorite shop, attaching a gift certificate and scheduling a date to come back together and choose something the recipient really wants.

One of my favorite ideas honors the spirit of the season by having children select an item to donate to another in need. This is a good opportunity to teach your children—and remind yourself—about the gift of generosity.

Please share your fortune at whatever level you are able. And talk to your kids about donating money and/or time to causes that matter to you.

Do Christmas cards stress you out? Don't send any then.

If you're like me, however, and cards are one of your favorite parts of the holidays, make the task enjoyable. Play Christmas music, drink eggnog and get together with your partner or a good friend and address them together.

Want to send cards, but can't seem to get them done in time? Not to worry. Send out Happy New Year cards instead.

Everyone celebrates the New Year. And here's a bonus: You'll have current addresses from the envelopes you collected!

Finally, savor the things that make this time of year unique. Bundle up and visit a local tree farm to pick out your tree. Hop in the car with some hot chocolate and take a ride through town to admire the lights. Check out events calendars and community bulletin boards for local events, plays, tree lightings and gatherings—yes, even caroling opportunities.

Here's wishing you more joy, less chaos and happy holidays to you and yours.

A grody kind of love

Love, it turns out, can be pretty gross. As much as I hate having the flu, it turns out there is something worse—watching my son go through it, while getting advice like, "Make sure he gets lots of rest and plenty of fluids."

Uh, OK. I'll be sure to let him know.

Although Sam and I survived his first projectile puke fest, it was traumatic, particularly for me. As he alternated between choking and spewing, he looked at me as if to say, "Why are you doing this to me? I thought you loved me?"

Kid, this is love. Who else would I hold against my body as they vomited into my hair and down my shirt?

No one. That's who.

My job as a grade school secretary prepared me to squelch my natural urge to add to the biohazard spill. But with other people's kids, all I had to do was offer some comfort and do some cleanup while I waited for the parent in charge to collect the sick kid.

This time, I was the parent in charge. And I didn't know what to do.

Despite my fear of seeming like a Munchausen mom, I called the pediatric triage nurse for the third time in a matter of days. She talked me back down to earth with some practical advice.

That reminds me of something. Since no one really wants to baby-sit your barfy child while you scour the supermarket for Pedialyte Freezer Pops, stash away some medicine, first aid supplies, shelf-stable juice and Pedialyte while you can.

Take a moment to program your pediatrician's number into your cell phone. And while you're at it, add the Poison Control hotline—1-800-222-1222.

When you call the national center, you'll be routed to a regional center where a helpful, nonjudgmental person will talk you through the worst-case scenario. Of course, it helps to have the container of the ingested item in hand when you dial.

I know all of this, because an hour after I typed the phone number into this column, Sam got into a bottle of lavender essential oil. When I tried to smell his breath, he tried to eat my nose.

Though you'll be asked a few questions, the calls are protected by the HIPAA privacy rule. So don't worry that you'll be seen as a bad parent.

Kids get into things. You learn from it and move on.

But do program the number in. It'll save time in an emergency.

Also, use caution gathering medical information online.

By the end of the evening, I was convinced Sam had one of three diseases, based on my medical degree by Google. It turned out he was just plain sick.

All joking aside, when in doubt, call the doctor's office. And be prepared to provide all necessary details to help the triage nurse assist you.

If you don't feel like you can call your pediatrician's office with questions, get a new one. Yes, I'm serious about that.

Take advantage of the "meet and greets" offered by many local doctors. You have the right to find a doctor you trust. Ask questions to see if the doctor shares some of your parenting philosophies.

Sam's pediatrician, the fabulous Dr. K, has helped us answer all kinds of parenting questions, on issues ranging from circumcision to vaccination and nutrition to sleep.

The bottom line is, kids get sick. Hopefully, you'll just be forking over the co-pay for some peace of mind. Either way, your pediatrician, nurses and support staff are your partners in parenting.

Just one more thing, as we emerge from the shared bowl of Chex Mix season. Don't forget to take extra good care of yourself. You know, get lots of rest and plenty of fluids.

Water-cooler for stay-at-home moms

FEB 3

Lately, I've been looking into forming some kind of union for stay-at-home moms. I'm thinking sick days, lunch and bathroom breaks, maybe even overtime pay. And one more thing: no more having the measure of my mothering weighed in the court of public opinion.

Mothering seems to be more susceptible to public criticism than most other jobs. For instance, with more than 3 billion minutes being spent on Facebook every day, by all kinds of people around the world, why did ABC News recently air a segment with this headline: "Does Facebook make you a bad mom?"

Are you kidding me? What about dads? What about employees and students?

Overindulging in anything from jogging to scrapbooking can take time away from other important activities. And since when are social connections unimportant?

Facebook, a social networking site offering a techy way of staying connected with folks, gives me a chance to take a minibreak. It lets me use big girl words and finish my sentences.

For the stay-at-home mom, Facebook is a virtual water-cooler.

Although I resent the question, I'll answer it: No, I don't think Facebook makes me a bad mom.

Is it easy to go overboard? Sure.

Initially, I have to admit, I was a bit of a Facebook freak. But I've scaled back to logging on a couple of times a day, while Sam is sleeping or busy chasing the dog around the living room.

Or is the dog chasing Sam? I don't know. I'm busy updating my Facebook page.

I can, however, still recognize the sound of silence, and thus reach the bathroom before the remote hits the bottom of the toilet. Usually anyway.

As with anything, Facebooking does pose a few problems. First, there's feeling that you're in a middle-school cafeteria as you wait for someone to "Friend" you back. Then, there's the issue of Facebook etiquette—assuming there is such a thing? Finally, there is Facebook envy.

If you've had it, you know what I'm talking about.

It's like this: Imagine opening yet another Christmas letter with a photograph of a color-coordinated family. Remember how you feel when you read letter after letter detailing trips to chateaus in places you can't pronounce? Well, Facebook envy is like getting those letters several times a day.

There you are wearing yoga pants, and not because you're doing any downward dogs, but because they still fit. And you have yogurt in your hair, of course.

When you look at pictures of the friends you used to have, still all cute and skinny and doing all sorts of fabulous things, it's easy to forget they're posting highlight reels, omitting the intervening fumbles.

On the upside, jealousy has a way of prompting you to tackle elements you are dissatisfied with in your life. After spending a little time reflecting on my Facebook envy, I realized there were a few things I could do differently.

I was envious of friends who looked terrific after having babies, so I joined a gym with day care service. I was jealous of friends who seemed to be having fun with their partners, actually going on dates sans bambinos, so I am so calling Sam's babysitter—soon.

Whatever it is you aren't satisfied with, it's up to you to fix it. That's the bad news, but it's also the good news.

Until I can get that union off the ground, it's up to me to do what works for me and my family, without regard to the public approval ratings.

Excuse me. I want to check my e-mail one more time before I wake Sam for snack time and another afternoon of dancing to "Yankee Doodle Dandy."

With kids, attitude is everything

MAR 4

It turns out that odd expression about little pitchers having big ears is true.

At first, it was adorable the way my son, Sam, started repeating after me.

"Good girl!" he says to the dog. "More?" he says to anyone with food. "Book!" he says as he gathers them in piles at my feet.

I found it so sweet—until he dropped a glass and said a word starting with "s" and ending with "t."

I can't even pretend to wonder where he learned it. I paused, holding my breath, thinking maybe I heard wrong.

"That's right, sit," I said, hopefully. He shook his head, pointed at the cup and repeated the expression.

Well, that's just great, I thought. Now I'll have to spell out my swear words, or, as my husband suggests, just stop swearing altogether.

I knew Sam was paying closer attention and mimicking my movements when I saw him get a stool, move it to the counter and then use the broom to bring something closer.

I'm a short person, so I'm constantly climbing up on stools or chairs or tables, and using whatever is handy to reach things, even if it's a butcher knife. I guess I'd better start modeling safer behavior, as I clearly never know what he's going to pick up.

In a broader sense, the attitudes and beliefs we impress on our children are paramount as they form their own perceptions of the world around them. This became clear to me while watching the news one evening.

Amid reports of all the various ways the sky is falling, I realized that if I wasn't careful, I might unintentionally raise my son in a culture of poverty consciousness. Since pretending there is no recession is teaching our kids to bury their heads in the sand, I suggest being real about the situation without burdening children with the responsibility of fixing it.

That doesn't mean kids can't help find solutions, though. Try asking your kids to identify places you can increase your family's bottom line, because spending less can be as helpful to your finances as earning more money.

You can make living leaner depressing and stressful or you can make it an adventure. For example, make a challenge for the whole family to see what kind of crazy meal concoctions you can create out of your cupboards.

While you don't want to teach children to fear money, you certainly want them to understand the value of it. Bottom line, attitude is everything.

It can be as simple as shifting from saying, "We can't afford that," to, "We've decided not to buy that right now." The difference might seem small, but it's profound.

Cultivating a good attitude costs nothing, but the rewards are priceless. Teaching your child to look for the good in every situation, even if it's the smallest of silver linings, is a life-long gift.

You might be surprised what kids pick up, so be open to listening to their feelings and fears.

Kids worry. They worry about where to sit in the cafeteria, who to play with at recess. They also worry about you.

Whether you're in a financial jam now or not, word of the recession is already out. It's making the rounds.

So talk to your kids. See what's on their mind.

As tempting as it might be, do not lie to your children. They can handle the truth as long as you equip them with the strength, grace and tools to do so.

Odds are, you're still working on being your best self. So am I.

But I suppose being a work in progress is a perfect example for our children, because it's real and it's honest.

Speaking of that, I'm thinking of starting a family "swear jar" to help with the cursing issue—or, more likely, create a nice little savings account.

Born tree-huggers

APR 1

I've loved words and writing for as long as I can remember. And I've hated math and science for an equally long time.

Luckily, serving as my son's tour guide to the planet has rejuvenated my interest in the sciences. But I must admit, I still feel intimidated by most things mathematical and all things scientific.

When people get to talking about the environment, carbon emissions, ozone gases and such, I tune out a bit. To be more accurate, I feel a twinge of guilt mixed with a dash of ignorance, and that typically leads me to check out of the conversation completely.

That isn't to say the importance of those issues is lost on me. I really just don't understand most of it, but here's what I do get: If we all start where we are now, and use whatever it is that motivates us to live greener, we can make an enormous difference.

It's fair to say most of us are motivated by a more tactile sort of "green."

Here's some good news. Going green has nothing to do with spending more of it.

I happen to be motivated by guilt as well. So it's no surprise that the first commitment I made to do my part for the planet was under duress.

It was in the late '80s when my brother eyed my mom as she threw away one of those six-pack plastic things. He dug it out of the trash and informed us of the dangers they pose to fish and seabirds.

My mom narrowed her eyes. "This is what they're teaching you at school," she asked, "that I kill fish?"

She started muttering in Slovak. She was wielding a meat cleaver, so we backed out of the kitchen.

To this day, I can't pass a plastic yoke in the garbage without taking scissors to it.

Parents of school-aged children be warned: Earth Day is coming April 22.

What do you do as a family for the environment? It might be a conversation worth having before your little darlings come running home from school with a Dixie cup full of dirt and seeds, ready to save the Earth.

Winning in the category of "Why Bother?" is Nickelodeon, for encouraging children to "unplug" from electronic gadgets on Earth Day —get this—for an entire minute. My favorite part is this: The one minute is scheduled for 9—at night.

In an age where children spend an average of six hours a day in front of an electronic screen, one minute is pretty weak sauce.

You can raise an environmentally conscious child even if you don't blow up your television, insist on soy-based crayons and rely exclusively on bamboo toys. Simply start with fresh air and getting a little dirt under your nails.

As I watch my son collect pine cones, chase feathers and delight in all things dirt, it occurs to me that children are natural little tree-huggers. Our job as parents is to nurture them in their exploration, foster their sense of wonder and teach them about respect.

The responsibility for making sure there's enough healthy planet to share with future generations belongs to all of us.

As with any group project, you're going to get varying levels of commitment and different degrees of interest, but that's OK. Even though we're in this together, it's still an "eyes on your own paper" kind of deal.

What you do for the environment matters and what you do to the environment matters. Whether you do more or less than your neighbor doesn't.

I know some environmental issues are contentious. I don't pretend to understand what I don't know much about.

I do, however, continue to do my homework. I trust we can all agree on the importance of managing our resources in order to leave trees for future generations—trees they can climb on and occasionally hug.

Here's to real moms—all of them

MAY 6

As calendars flip to May and bouquets of flowers begin to pop up in grocery stores, I cringe a bit. I know what's coming the second Sunday of the month: Mother's Day.

I can't think of a more emotionally loaded holiday.

Long before I became a mom myself, this May holiday made me feel all twisted up inside. All the macaroni necklaces, crumbs in bed and homemade coupons in the world couldn't quite sum up the gratitude I felt for my mom.

Last year, my first as a mom, I realized the day wasn't about grand gestures and fancy displays of affection.

In my life before Sam, paychecks used to come every other Friday. Now, they come in the currency of sticky fingers around my neck and sweet, sloppy kisses.

Mother's Day, as I see it, is the annual payday to express love and thanks. It is also a day for me to celebrate how blessed I am to have the opportunity to be a mother.

According to the mom salary wizard at Salary.com, my worth as a mother is $168,503.00 a year.

Of course, this paycheck is printed on computer paper rather than dollar bills. And it doesn't factor in overtime, working through breaks and being on call all night.

Still, it's a nice idea to try to determine the value of a mother. Except that, of course, you can't. Not really. This paper paycheck is a bit amusing, but parenting is one of those gigs you can't put a price on.

Being a "real" mom, by the way, has little to do with how you got the job and everything to do with how you go about doing it.

On Mother's Day in 1990, I found out I was adopted. That little tidbit complicated the holiday for me until recently, when I made contact with my birth mother for the first time.

Let's just say it didn't go quite as well as I'd hoped, but didn't go quite as badly as I'd feared. More than anything, I felt relieved to know I didn't just hatch, even though my birth mother didn't want to meet me.

I never felt like I was looking for my "real" mom, as many suggested. It was always clear to me who that was: my Mami.

My real mom is the one who loved me before she met me. She's the one who changed my diapers, spoon-fed me bananas, took me to the library, taught me to return my books on time and drove me to college in an over-packed minivan. She's the one who loved me in all my crazy hair colors and styles, then paid to have my hair stripped out when the "temporary" colors didn't fade in time for our Christmas pictures.

I have a tremendous amount of gratitude for my biological mother, of course, for giving me the opportunity to have this life. But on Mother's Day, it's my real mom who gets my cards and tokens of appreciation—the mom, I am certain, who was meant to be my mom from the beginning.

While I always understood that not all of us meet our mothers in the hospital delivery room, I couldn't be completely positive until I knew for my own self that my pregnancy hardly factors into the love I feel for my son. In fact, memories from that ordeal actually count against him, what with all the middle of the night rib-kicking and bladder stomping.

The poor little guy.

I started plotting my revenge during hour 13 of labor. By hour 23, with him still refusing to emerge, I began imagining myself chaperoning his school dances—all of them.

Luckily, Sam was born shortly afterward. So our scorecard remains roughly even.

Instead of that paper paycheck for $168,503.00, I'd prefer a toast to not trying to put a value on the job of mothering. I'd gratefully settle for breakfast in bed and a noodle necklace.

I cherish this job, even though it takes all of my heart and all of my energy all of the time. And for that level of commitment, I relish the chance to bask in a day of pampering and affection.

For future reference, because I am clipping these for Sam's scrapbook, I also expect my son to pick out his own cards and come up with his own gestures of gratitude, even if he is clever enough to marry a woman willing to do it for him.

This year, as the calendar turns to May, I toast all mothers. I say cheers to macaroni necklaces, homemade coupons and not enough words.

About that memo on parenting ...

JUN 3

I know it's hard to keep track of things with a busy toddler underfoot, but I can't find this memo all the other mothers seem to have gotten on proper etiquette for parenting in public.

When I first started taking Sam to public parks last summer, I had a vague sense I was breaking unspoken rules.

When we hit the story-time circuit, I realized it wasn't just me. Parenting in public can be so painful and awkward that some just opt out of taking their children to public places in order to avoid the judgment.

Being Sam's mom is like having front row seats to a show called, "Which of these is not like the others?" Take, for example, our first experience with toddler storytime at the public library.

All the other children seemed to understand it was time to settle down and put on their listening ears, except this one little blond boy. He refused to sit in my lap, preferring instead to inspect his surroundings.

I let him have at it. By some of the looks I got, the etiquette memo must have directed otherwise.

I wish that was as bad as it got.

At one point, Sam decided to pick a foreign object off the floor and, naturally, pop it in his mouth. As I dug it out, I felt his body stiffen in his signature "I'm about to throw a tantrum" move.

I took him outside to let him have his fit. I figured I wasn't giving the choking hazard back and he wasn't going to ruin story time for anyone else.

He pitched his fit, then got distracted looking at the other kids through the window, so we went back in.

No worries, except for the horrified looks I kept getting from Ms. Judgey McJudgington. She looked at me as if I were beating the kid.

What's funny is that if I hadn't taken him outside, I know I would've gotten the same feedback from someone else.

When she nodded in my direction and said something to her friend, who turned to look, and I felt 12 again. I was so humiliated, I didn't want to come back.[*]

But the thing is, I love the library. I want my son to love books as much as his parents do. I think spending time there, indoor voice or not, is important.

So we tried the "Busy Hands and Feet" session, and we found it more our style. Thankfully, the teacher was patient.

All went well until she announced the children were to play a game where they put all the instruments back into the box. Uh-oh.

I watched Sam grin as all the children put things back into the box for him to pull out.

The teacher eventually persuaded him to give up his tambourine and let her close the box. But he watched her like a hawk and noted where she put it away.

Then, and this is the part that scares me, he waited until she got busy with the next activity, then he made a beeline for the instrument box.

We had to take a little time out before getting back in on the action. Only this time, I wasn't alone.

I guess that's just how the "Busy Hands and Feet" folks roll.

I suppose I'll get thicker skin eventually. In the meantime, it helps to realize this: Kids will throw fits, people will look askance and the sun will still rise in the morning. If you're one of those who got the memo, though, would you send it my way?

---

[*] It occurs to me, years later, that perhaps they weren't talking about me at all. But as a work-in-progress myself I've only recently cultivated the habit of jumping to positive conclusions. Before, everything seemed personal - and not in a good way. But now, I figure if I'm jumping to conclusions and making stuff up in my head, it might as well be good stuff. This is way more fun. But that lady back then was talking about me. I'm pretty sure. But really, so what?

Bliss turns to terror in a blink

JUL 1

Parenting has its moments, doesn't it? Lots of them: sweet ones, crazy ones, some you never want to forget and others you wish you could.

Some of my all-time favorite moments with my 20-month old son involve swimming. Of course, by swimming I mean holding on tightly to something akin to a squirming, splashing baby seal. Pure bliss.

Neither of us was afraid of the water until we were schooled last weekend in how quickly bliss can turn into terror. Did you know a child can drown in the time it takes to answer the phone? Or, that according to the Centers for Disease Control and Prevention, Oregon is one of 10 states where drowning surpasses all other causes of death to children age 14 and under?

And here's one more sobering statistic from the Orange County Fire Authority in California, "of all preschoolers who drown, 70 percent are in the care of one or both parents at the time of the drowning." I suppose I'm in good company, then, because when Sam slipped facedown into a friend's pool this weekend, I was standing right there.

What kid hasn't been asked what they'd do if their friends jumped off the (insert name of local bridge)? For me, it was the Tacoma Narrows Bridge and I always assured Mom that I would not jump. And yet, here I am a mother and I gave in, against my gut instinct, and let my kid do what other kids were doing so that I didn't seem mean.

I'd been trying to keep Sam busy playing inside while he watched his little friends playing near the pool. There were balls in the pool. I know my son. He's like our Labrador. Nothing gets between him and his desire to get a ball. Which will serve him well on the field someday but as a fully dressed toddler near a swimming pool? Not so much.

I let him outside to play anyway. I warned him that if he tried to get in the pool even once we would leave immediately.

"That is so mean!" I heard someone exclaim. Is it? How many warnings should I give when it comes to something as important as life or death? It didn't take long before the wind carried his ball into the pool, just out of reach. He went after it, tripping over his titch-too-big Tevas and landing in the pool. Face first. Watching his little body floating there was one of the worst moments in my life. The world went mute as I went in after him.

"Breathe!" I heard my voice pleading. I held him against me, both of us soaked, and listened to him breathe. As soon as I knew he was OK, I did what any normal mother would do. I freaked out.

As my friend took care of Sam, I took a moment to lose it completely, collect myself and change into dry clothes. I found Sam bundled up in dry towels and propped up on my friends' cushy bed. They were watching Motocross, Sam leaning forward watching the bikes make laps around the muddy tracks. "Bike, vroom! Vroom! Bike!"

All the way home I kept going over what happened. I let some stranger's opinion of me get in the way of ensuring my son's safety. What was I thinking? How in the world are we going to get to preschool safely, much less through high school and beyond?

Sam seemed to be playing a different tape in his mind. There in the backseat, I saw him grinning ear to ear, "vroom! vroom! vroom! Mama, bike?"

Since then, I hug Sam a little tighter, watch a little closer and concern myself less with what others think. Also, I've added worrying about whether or not he'll remember to wear his helmet on rides when he's older to my list of things that keep me up at night. Oh, and I plan to take a CPR refresher course this summer. Other than that, we'll see you at the pool.

Tales of a 2 1/2-foot terrorist

AUG 5

Just when I started to feel as if I was getting a handle on this whole parenting gig, two things made me wonder if I would ever feel that way again: Sam discovered the art of throwing tantrums and I began puking for a good cause.

I realized how insane these new developments might be when the 70 pounds of Labrador attached to my right hand and the 30 pounds of toddler attached to my left hand both refused to budge. With my 16-weeks-pregnant belly leading the way, and my bright red face, I could only imagine what people were thinking: And she's going to add a baby to this mayhem?

I sure am.

The little one is due in January, making it a Capricorn like its daddy. So there will be no shortage of stubbornness in the Hardy house.

I'm mostly thrilled at the thought of a new person joining our family. But I'm also terrified at being outnumbered by adorable but needy little people.

Sam has recently developed one awful, one adorable and one alarming habit.

First, we've moved into the tantrum-throwing phase of our relationship.

Second, he's begun asking for and giving the sweetest hugs. He'll hug us, our dog, his stuffed animals, a stranger at the library and his reflection in the oven door.

Now for the alarming part: At 21 months, he's learned to use hugs to get what he wants.

When crying, squirming and screaming "ALL DONE!" doesn't work to get him out of the grocery cart, he'll wait a little while, then sweetly ask for a hug. How do you say no to that?

Once he has his Cheerio-dust-coated hands wrapped tightly around my neck, he refuses to let go. He insists on having his clever self picked up.

If you've seen us shopping around town, you know who wins. I'm the disheveled mom pushing a cart with my hip and forearm while balancing Sam and his trifecta of security: giraffe, blanket and water bottle in the other.

Otherwise, I try to maintain a firm policy against negotiating with 2 1/2-foot terrorists. As worn down as I get by these new back-arching, head-banging tantrums, I still insist on the "no playing with knives" and "no running out into the street" rules.

Parents have to pick their battles, though.

I've come to realize there is no harm in some behaviors of Sam's that might seem bizarre. Embarrassment maybe, but no harm.[*]

So I let Sam go about town carrying not one but three spatulas, while sporting a necklace and plastic knight hat. I get funny looks and occasional comments, but I figure the adornments are cheap, relatively safe and noise-free.

With Sam about to have his little "I'm the center-of-the-Universe" world rocked, I thought I'd help him ease into his new big brother role by bringing out the Cabbage Patch Kids of my childhood. Sam watched intently as I introduced him to Joseph Marvin and Mala Suzy.

I showed him how to hold a doll gently, then gave him a chance to emulate me.

For a moment, Sam appeared to be drawing Joseph Marvin close for a hug. But as I reached for my camera, he pounded the doll's face against the shelf and then hurled him to the floor.

When he reached for Mala Suzy, I offered him a spatula instead. Maybe we'll try dolls again another day.

---

[*] As an interesting aside: it took some time for me to figure this out but Sam's truly terrible episodes ceased completely when I discovered they were linked to red dye consumption and removed it from his diet, which is trickier than you'd think given it's in everything from teething medicine to chocolate. I have much more to say about this and will, someday.

PSA: What not to say

OCT 7

Somewhere in the middle of my first bout of pregnancy, I got so frustrated with the rude, personal comments and questions from strangers that I promised myself if there ever was a round two, I'd just lie a lot.

It turns out, the comments are different this time around. Except, unfortunately, for my personal favorite: "Wow! You're huge!"

Consider this article sort of a public service announcement on how to talk to a pregnant woman without getting a hormone-fueled tongue lashing, or at least avoid some awkwardness and hurt feelings. I'm aware that we live in a reality television, tell-all, bare-all world, but really people, some things are better left unsaid. Here are a few of them.

Let's start with something I wish went without saying.

Attention friends, family and strangers at Safeway: No pregnant woman wants to hear how big she looks. Ever. Just trust me on this.

While we're on the subject, as sure as you might be that all the medical professionals overseeing my pregnancy somehow missed the "rest" of the babies during my ultrasounds, try to refrain from insisting that there's just "no way" I'm "this big" with "just one baby." I could start a trust fund if I had a nickel for every time I've heard this.

Since weight gain is one of the given and visible delights of pregnancy, I should also warn you that if you insist on knowing exactly how much weight I've gained—"No, really, how much?"—ask at your own risk. And for the love of all that is holy, please refrain from asking in front of a group of people.

Also, if I tell you I'm having a boy and you are of the evidently common opinion that I should be having a girl because I already have a boy, please keep your disappointment to yourself. Please avoid offering me unsolicited and unnecessary consolation lines like, "At least he's healthy," or, "At least you don't have to buy anything."

Since learning I'm the proud prospective mama of Yamhill County's own Hardy boys, I've been surprised at how many times people have asked if I'm disappointed.

Seriously? Isn't the real blessing of parenting having the opportunity to serve as a 24-7 tour guide as our children, regardless of gender, grow into themselves?

My 2-year-old son seemed to be the only one who didn't have an opinion on the gender of his future sibling.

Moments before the big ultrasound, I asked Sam if he wanted a brother or a sister. He said: "Lawnmower."

And finally, no list of pregnancy pet peeves would be complete without this request dating back to preschool: Please keep your hands to yourself.

While there may be a few pregnant women who won't agree with me on this, I think I speak for most of us when I say we don't want our stomachs touched any more than you do.

Despite the resemblance, I'm not Buddha incarnate. I can't grant you good luck in exchange for a belly rub.

Frankly, I would prefer to avoid the awkward moment altogether. If you feel the need to reach out and rub a tummy, at least ask for permission.

I don't mean to give the impression that it's safer to just back away slowly when you see a pregnant woman. Just the opposite, actually.

I enjoy talking with strangers and hearing stories about their experiences with pregnancy and parenting. I just thought it might be helpful to share this condensed version of what not to say or touch in case it spares you, or the pregnant woman in line behind you, any awkwardness.

On behalf of those of us waddling around all hormonal until our babies make it safely into the world, thank you for taking this under advisement.

Common sense for an uncommon flu season

NOV 4

With nightly news reports on swine flu and the raging health care debate, it's easy to feel powerless over our own health.

Truth is, we might get sick. Some of us will even get really, really sick while others will escape the flu altogether and chalk "swine flu" up there with the "Y2K" panic of 1999. Either way, with proper planning and prevention, we do have some control over what happens to us and how we handle it.

Being pregnant just happens to put me in one of the "high risk" categories for this particular pandemic, which has resulted in many well-meaning people reminding me of the potential risks to me and my developing baby. Initially, I freaked out and started pricing anti-contamination suits.

Eventually, though, I decided that it's more dangerous for me and the baby to live in a perpetual state of anxiety, and that it's even worse to raise my son to believe the world is not safe. Yes, we might get sick but we'll take care of each other and this too shall pass.

Meanwhile, my son continues his love of licking random objects and recently developed the darling habit of putting his finger in his nose. Despite, or perhaps because of, these things we practice common sense prevention techniques: good hand washing (which nearly always leads to one of us getting drenched and having to change our clothes), coughing and sneezing into the crook of our elbows (this we're trying to teach by example, but it's a tricky concept for a toddler) and minimizing physical contact with others (don't be surprised when Sam offers you the new "healthier" handshake, aka the fist bump) and, of course, eating nutritiously.

Despite our best prevention efforts, odds are in favor of the flu raiding our house at some point in the next few months. Unannounced and unwelcome as it is, I want to be ready when this houseguest comes to visit.

So I start with keeping my toilets clean enough to puke in. Trust me, with all the causes my bleeding heart has taken up, it is a surprise even to me that I'm such an advocate for clean toilets. But ever since my son discovered all the magic that happens behind that child-proofed bathroom doorknob, his little hands have touched parts of the toilet I never used to even consider cleaning.

I recently discovered I could save a chunk of change by using natural, cheaper cleaning solutions, like mixing a cup of vinegar with one-quarter cup of baking soda. I learned the hard way to mix this concoction in a container large enough to handle the fizzing and overflow. But you probably paid closer attention in your chemistry classes than I did. Your toddler, on the other hand, will love all the bubbles resulting in "Mama's mess."

While I'm doling out advice I'd have no place giving in my pre-mom life, may I recommend keeping an extra set of clean sheets, pajamas and blanket at the ready? After surviving the trauma of my son's first puke-a-rama last year, I'm haunted by the memory of hunting for clean pajamas and sheets while still dripping from, well, you know.

Since the last place you need to be when you're sick is roaming the aisles of the supermarket for chicken soup and crackers, stock up soon on your sick must-haves like over-the-counter medicines, Pedialyte pops, thermometers, tissues, chicken noodle soup, sprite and crackers. Really soon. Like on your next trip to the grocery store.

While we can't control how all of Congress votes on health care, and we can't stop swine flu from being an issue, maybe some of these suggestions will help keep your family healthier, or at least more comfortable, during these next few months.

And, hopefully, all you get sick of this flu season is hearing about it.

Parenting is a moving target

DEC 2

New realities should play into decisions .

Along with the joys and tidings of this time of year, there's no shortage of stress and potentially awkward moments. Like, say, when your kid gets a gift that makes you cringe.

When it comes to parenting, it's inevitable for values to collide. How you handle these occasions is key in maintaining healthy relationships with family and friends.

Recently, Sam's Nana and Papa brought him the cutest pair of pajamas printed with little brown Labradors resembling our Lucy Brown. Sam calls them "Good Girl jammies."

He was especially excited about the matching fleece robe. He still strolls around the house, hands tucked casually into his pockets, like a little Hugh Hefner wannabe in search of an ascot.

Nana and Papa also brought toy wooden guns for Sam. This created a different kind of excitement.

In their defense, Matt's parents meant to ask us how we felt about it in advance, but Sam saw them first. Matt managed the classic "hide and distract" maneuver and a conversation between the adults ensued.

My husband and I grew up with different ideas about a lot of things, including guns.

For him, rural life included a healthy respect for guns. For me, growing up in Tacoma, guns were something gang members had; I was terrified of them.

Before I was a parent—cue laugh track—I was certain I'd be the "no guns for us" kind of mom. But the more I talk to people about guns, the more I realize it's important to me to teach my children what they are, how to use them and why I don't ever want them to have to pull a trigger in a hostile situation. I realize I can't ban guns completely.

Although it's not unusual for me and my father-in-law to come at something from opposite points of view, we are getting better at finding the middle and lowering our voices along the way.

He mentioned that he grew up playing with all manner of toy guns, and he turned out fine.

But he grew up in a different setting. He grew up in a country that didn't have the phrases "school shootings," "went postal," and "Columbine" in its regular lexicon.

The reality today, according to the American Academy of Pediatrics, is that more than 40 percent of American homes with children in them include guns, many of which are kept loaded and unlocked. In a world where an American child under the age of 10 is killed or disabled by a gun every other day, according to the AAP, I think it's fair for a parent to be concerned about the issue.

That being said, it's also necessary to keep the spirit of the gift-giver in mind and be tactful in handling gift situations.

If there's something you feel strongly about, I suggest you have a conversation in advance with potential gift-givers. Feel free to use our awkward moment as a segue to preventing your own.

Ultimately, we decided to keep the toy guns. We agreed that a conversation prior to having them in the house would've been helpful, but we let Sam take a turn with them.

He thought they were "pretty cool" as he used them as makeshift hockey sticks. They are now tucked away until we've figured out how we want to handle gun-play.

I'm not looking for Mayberry. I'm just saying that parents today can't make their decisions based on what our parents and grandparents did, simply because they turned out OK.

Using some of the common sense that seemed more prevalent in prior generations, however, isn't such a bad idea.

When someone gives us a gift, we say thank you. If the gift comes into conflict with our values, talk about it respectfully and see if you can't find a middle ground.

Isn't that, after all, what you're raising your kids to do?

To remember is sublime, to forget divine

JAN 6

Until recently, I wondered what was up with the forgetfulness of parents who'd gone before me. Like my mom, who doesn't remember me crying in the middle of the night. Ever. Or friends who, when grilled for specifics, can't remember how they handled challenging logistics like traveling with toddlers.

It seems the details of life with newborns get suspiciously and quickly forgotten. I'm sure this is why well-meaning people do things like insist new moms "sleep while the baby sleeps" and the baby simply needs [insert piece of advice the new parent has tried repeatedly and unsuccessfully].

The baby, by the way, sleeps while you're doing the grocery shopping or out on the road somewhere, not when you're ready to call it a night. That brings me to one of the earliest and most hilarious misconceptions I had about what new motherhood would be like.

I had a vision, which I now know was more of a lovely daydream, of my fingers flying across the keyboard as I met my freelance deadlines while my sweet baby slept soundly in a bassinet beside me. I am only now ready to laugh about how far from reality that turned out to be.

I also had some misconceptions of what my husband and I would be like as new parents. I had this romantic notion of us gazing adoringly at each other over the top of our sleeping darling.

First of all, there was more glaring than gazing in those initial weeks. Second, there was very little sleeping, which I'm sure had a direct correlation to the aforementioned glaring.

At the time of this writing, I'm 38 weeks pregnant. And I find myself on the verge of turning everything upside down again after finally having found my balance as a mother to my now 2-year-old son, Sam.

This is how I've come to suspect these gaps in parental memories are perhaps biologically necessary for propagation of the human race.

The first two years of Sam's life have already blurred together into a fuzzy haze of mostly rosy memories. Luckily or not, though, I took notes.

I'd forgotten, for example, how extremely frustrated I was—and am again—by the fact that with all the advances in medicine and technology, the best we can do at predicting an event as important as the impending birth of a child is this maddening sentence: "After (insert any one of a number of disgusting signs of labor here) happens, you might have the baby between now and oh, say, two weeks." That's terrific.

I was surprised to flip through my notes from those early months with Sam and find just how much I'd already forgotten. Like, for instance, the way I used to scramble to get Sam out of his bassinet and nurse him by the light of my open cell phone, clenching it in my teeth by the antenna.

My husband had an hour-long commute in a few short hours, and I didn't want to risk waking him by turning a light on. But this time, I'm springing for a night light.

I also forgot how worried I was about not having all the answers, or even most of them. Now I'm certain that's why God made Google.

Despite what I now consider species-preservational amnesia, I feel I'm going into this second round better prepared for the reality of life with an infant.

There will be mayhem. There will be meltdowns. And there will be a time I long for these days again.

Meanwhile, I just have to remember that it's really OK that some days, my biggest accomplishment will be that the kids are partially dressed and the dishwasher partially unloaded.

Lessons learned in labor of love

FEB 3

A couple of weeks ago, I woke up at 5 a.m. with instructions to call a specific number to see if there was room at the inn, so to speak. As soon as I got the green light, my husband and I loaded our overnight bags into the car and checked in at our destination.

While it sounds like we were going on vacation, we were actually going to the birthing center of our local hospital, which is nice, but not exactly Barbados.

Childbirth is nothing short of a miracle, I'll give you that. There are, however, quite a few other adjectives I'd use to describe it as well.

I'll spare you what I consider the grosser, better left forgotten details. Instead, I'll share a few things I learned during this labor of love.

First, let's address birthing plans.

A birthing plan, by definition, seems to be a document first-time pregnant women are encouraged to write in order to give them the illusion of control over the whole labor and delivery gig.

Turns out, it's nice to have an idea of how you want things to go, and you should by all means discuss your wishes with your medical team. But you should bear in mind that everything is subject to change, so your best bet is to go with the flow.

You might consider making that your motto for the next 18 years anyway.

Perhaps even more important than flexibility is having faith. I'm convinced that confidence in your medical team, your labor partner and, above all, yourself are essential to creating a positive birthing experience. One of the most incredible things about having had the opportunity to experience childbirth for myself is getting to tap into this inner reserve of strength I never knew I had.

In fact, I always thought I was a bit of a wuss. It turns out I'm kind of a rock star.

In addition to helping me grow a healthy, happy, good sleeper to term, and deliver him into the world, my obstetrician, the awesome Dr. Barker, reminded me of what is perhaps most important to remember as a new mother. His parting words after our son's birthday party were a reminder to ask for what I need.

This is not the time to be a hero, rock-star status aside. I am forever grateful to the lovely nurses who brought kindness to my bedside around-the-clock, in the form of pain relief, ice-cold water, fresh nightgowns, nursing advice and food on a tray that was wheeled away when I was done picking at it.

Finally, I highly encourage dads and labor partners to BYOB. That last "b" is for bed.

Also, please pack snacks. The hospital cafeteria offers great food, but is closed nights and weekends.

Matt tried to make himself comfortable on the little joke-bed, but every time he turned, it sounded like a circus clown's horn. I heard my husband mutter from across the room: "This bed is ridiculous." He said something about being uncomfortable.

Um.

I assured him that despite the fact that my bed had a bunch of controls to make me more comfortable, it wasn't exactly like anyone was bringing me drinks with tiny umbrellas in them.

The cost of our little stay at the hospital might shake out to the equivalent of a long tropical cruise. But instead of coming home with a tan and smuggled rum, we've got something way better.

His name is Jacob Henry Hardy. He weighed in at 9 pounds, 12 ounces, and he's every bit as awesome as we could've imagined.

Welcome to the world, Baby Jake, and thank you Dr. Barker, Natasha Lawson, the amazing and patient medical staff and all the wonderful people at Willamette Valley Medical Center for your part in making this dream come true.

Take pride in 'mama' medals

MAR 3

I nearly submitted a column of record-breaking brevity this month. I had just five words in mind: "This page intentionally left blank."

When my editor called to ask me if I'd lost my mind, I figured I could pass it off as an ironic portrayal of my life as the mother of both a toddler and a newborn—a page out of a life where writing seems to be limited to lists of questions for the doctor and checks made out to the hospital.

But then something kind of cool happened.

The day after watching Shaun White win another gold medal snowboarding in the half-pipe, I mentioned to a friend how much I admired his mad tricks, raw talent and pure enthusiasm. "I wish I could be as awesome as Shaun White at anything," I said, "even for a day."

"You are," my friend answered, pointing to the boys. "The Olympics are just games. This is real life, only there's no spotlight."

As I sat there with the baby's fresh spit-up in my hair, most of Sam's dinner in my lap and hormones still going crazy in my body, I got a little choked up. As small as it may seem, in a job where guilt and criticism are all too common, there's no such thing as too many compliments.

As I basked in the warmth of my friend's praise, it felt a little like someone had draped an imaginary medal around my neck.

I haven't mastered the McTwist. And I'd never heard of a "double cork" before I Googled "Shaun White."

But come to think of it, I suppose I could qualify to compete in the Olympics with a few tricks of my own. I'd proudly compete in speed-showering, toddler-wrangling and tandem diaper-changing.

Since I know I'm not alone in an under-appreciated field of work, I got to thinking about comedian Bill Engvall's "Here's your sign" campaign, warning people they were about to come into contact with stupidity. It was embraced by enough people that I'm thinking we could start our own version—more helpful, albeit less humorous.

I have in mind a "Here's your medal" movement. If you see a parent doing something you respect, tell them. It's that simple.

It'll help make up for all the times they have to skulk out of the store for taking their toddler in too close to nap time. Or is that just me?

We spend our time sweeping Cheerios instead of events. So we are ultimately judged by our conscience—and our children—instead of placards held up by a panel of experts.

While the Olympic torch is extinguished during the closing ceremonies, the torch we light for our children never goes out. Instead, it burns in our hearts forever, lighting a path through the darker times of parenting.

For parents, victory isn't a game. It isn't even something tangible. Victory for me has nothing to do with triple axles or signature tricks.

I celebrate moments when I manage to get my kids to sleep simultaneously or see Sam share his toys without being asked. Sometimes, a win around here is simply persuading Sam to sit still at the dinner table and actually eat some of his food.

Getting a column done on deadline, with no child care, requires typing most of it with one hand. Now that's the kind of victory I'm proud to celebrate.

It's not the life of a super-star athlete. No one is singing the national anthem in my honor.

But I wear my "mama" medals proudly. I hope you'll join me in passing on the gold.

Liar, liar, mama's on fire: but don't put it out

APR 7

I recently read a shocking statistic: Only 80 percent of parents lie to their children. Isn't it actually 100 percent?

Lying is such an ugly word, though. I think of it more as creative problem-solving.

Take, for example the following things my toddler, Sam, loves to eat:

"More ice cream!" No problem. For breakfast? Sure. I give Sam ice cream whenever he wants it, because to him, that just means ice cubes in his water.

"More cake, please!" No problem. At our house, "cakes" are veggie patties.

"More shake, Mama!" Coming right up, because it's loaded with all kinds of healthy stuff and lots of ice cream (see above).

Admittedly, I once had a little lying problem. Back in grade school, I got on this kick of telling outrageous stories, like pretending I was Punky Brewster's cousin.

My lies didn't hurt anyone—except me, when I was humiliated at Sara Stillman's birthday.

It seems her mother couldn't resist calling me out on my then-current whopper—that my parents kept adopting more kids and we couldn't afford to send them all to school.

I learned my lesson about lying that afternoon. I stayed away from it until one day, while on a long trip, when my toddler freaked out because his helicopter disappeared.

"But look at all the water-copters, Sam!" I said hopefully. He sucked in his breath like he does when he's excited.

"Water-copters!" I have to admit, I felt a little rush at the ease with which the lie came to me—and how well it worked. We hunted for water-copters the rest of the way.

Luckily it was summer and we were driving through farm country. So irrigation guns were abundant.

Someday Sam will discover that our television doesn't stay broken for hours on end, then suddenly decide to work again when I want him to sit still for 11 minutes while I shave my left leg in peace.

Right now, however, "broken" is a concept that works better for him than a lecture on the television guidelines established by the American Academy of Pediatrics. Plus, he likes to fix broken things with his tools, and that can buy me enough time to shave my right leg.

When faced with a 2-year-old falling apart over not having any juice, why not use my mommy superpowers to turn plain water into refrigerator juice? Life has plenty of disappointments, and my kid is certainly familiar with the word "no," but whenever I can create a win-win situation with a creative white lie, why not?

Spoiler alert: Tooth Fairy? Santa Claus? The bunny with the candy-filled eggs that somehow symbolizes the resurrection of Jesus Christ? All lies.

But they're the kind I'm happy to tell until the magic fades away.

For the same reason, I don't argue with Sam about whether or not it really was Giraffe who threw the toy car. I just give Giraffe a timeout, figuring everyone will learn the intended lesson.

Am I a shameless liar? Or am I an unapologetic mom blessed with superpowers that transform "gross" vegetables into delectable desserts by changing nothing other than what we call it?

The truth about parents is that we're in pretty good company, with 80 percent of us admitting to it. As for the other 20 percent, I have to wonder if their noses didn't grow just a little when they said they never tell a lie.

School brings lessons for mom

MAY 5

Maybe it was a bit ambitious of me, so soon after Jake was born, to sign up to be somewhere on time twice a week. But enrolling Sam in pre-preschool turned out to be an even better decision than I could have imagined.

Initially, I wanted something just for Sam as he adjusted to the idea of this little interloper we kept calling his brother. I also thought it wouldn't hurt for him to get used to taking direction from someone besides his parents.

As an added bonus, this commitment gave me the impetus to work out the logistical challenges of getting two kids out the door, into the car and back out of the car much earlier than I did with Sam.

What I didn't know when I signed us up for pre-preschool was that I was actually going to be the one getting "schooled." My first big lesson was to think twice about how I explained things to Sam.

The day before he was to start, we had an at-home consultation with Sandy Tuck, the fabulous dog trainer, for our little Houdini. I explained to Sam that Lucy was going to school.

I've never seen the kid's eyes as wide as they were when he wandered into the room just as Sandy was standing on Lucy's leash to encourage her into a settle position. In retrospect, I probably shouldn't have called it school.

Then again, Sam was amazingly well behaved his first day.

Looking back on the pictures, I wish I'd thought to run a comb through his hair before we left the house. But at the time, I was just thrilled we all had pants on—and shoes.

That brings me to the next lesson: Forcing your child to wear appropriate shoes for school is a battle worth fighting.

Perhaps I was a little worn down from the whole business of nursing a newborn round the clock. But when Sam insisted on wearing his too-big cowboy boots to school, I let him.

Sam promptly tripped over his boots and chipped a tooth. While I had Sam in a wrestling hold in the dentist's chair, I noticed he'd also developed a goose egg on his head.

How did that happen? Note to self: Check the whole kid out after the next injury.

I learned another safety lesson when I heard the "click" of my car doors locking with my keys, and children, inside. My car happened to be parked across the street from the sheriff's office. I was relieved when Sam finally accepted the lollipop bribe to unlock the doors, just as the deputies were crossing the parking lot toward us.

I learned that paint comes out of hair, that Sam is old enough to play with scissors made for kids and that yogurt, even in stick form, is a terrible idea in the car. Perhaps most importantly, I discovered that it only seems like everyone else is more organized.

Truthfully, I'm starting to get the feeling we're all just winging it. It's our attitude that determines whether we come across as "with it" or "out of it."

It took me three weeks to get us to school on time. Imagine my surprise to find the only other person in the room was the teacher.

I enjoyed being in an environment where it was perfectly acceptable to talk about potty-training ideas, and to compare notes on how much, or how little, sleep we got the night before. And Sam learned to equate learning with fun.

I constantly find myself channeling the phenomenally patient and kind Ms. Amanda during my day-to-day toddler interactions. I am eternally thankful to my son's first teacher for laying the foundation for a successful education and—whether she knew it or not—teaching me how to be a better mother.

Playing the good mom, bad mom game

I had a little Facebook fiasco recently.

My husband said I could've avoided the drama if I hadn't cared so much what people think. But it would have arisen eventually, because any mom who puts herself out there, whether by posting a status update on her children or by simply taking her kids out in public, risks being on the receiving end of stinging criticism.

Of course, I increase my odds by writing about parenting, both in print here and on my blog. So, I suppose it was just a matter of time.

Did you know moms are reported to be among the meanest people on the Internet?

It just so happens that my little Facebook fight occurred within a day of ABC's airing of a Good Morning America segment titled, "Mean Moms." And it's so true that the isolation of the Internet fosters hyper-hostility.

Even though I always put my real name on anything I write, online or otherwise, I still find myself reacting more harshly to online attitude than I might to some of the smug, judgmental attitudes prevalent on playgrounds and other places where mothers meet in person.

When I'm lucky enough to beat the boys awake, I catch a quick shower and hop online while mainlining some caffeine. The morning of the aforementioned incident, I found a chiropractor friend had posted a link to an article highlighting the safety concerns of some commonly used baby gear, three elements of which I had within few feet of my computer.

I respect her personally, as a mother with a baby the same age as mine, as well as professionally. But her parenting path is paved with, shall we say, more organic materials than mine. Frankly, my road has been littered with good intentions, but also with plastic, chemicals and sometimes processed food.

I spent the better part of the morning eyeing my baby in his various "containers," wondering if I really was sacrificing his development in the name of entertainment (his) and convenience (mine). I wouldn't call myself a lazy mom, but rather your average two-handed one.

The nagging feeling that I was somehow harming my children stayed with me. After the boys went down for an afternoon nap, I re-

read the article for alternatives to the ExerSaucer, and I noticed some people had weighed in on this surprisingly controversial subject.

In the few seconds it took to scan the comments, I felt personally attacked. Even though the Internet evokes a sense of anonymity, real people read your words and their reactions have an impact.

One mom explained why she shunned the use of ExerSaucers. "It's a commitment, because you have to put in the extra time to actually watch your kid. But hey, I think that's what they call parenting."

That's when I got a little insane.

Here my friend had posted something that was interesting to her, and instead of being able to have a real conversation with her about differing opinions and parenting methods, I got this overwhelming sense those of us who did things differently were under attack as "uneducated" and "neglectful." I'm not putting words in people's mouths, or keyboards, by the way. Those are quotes.

I responded by posting a comment of my own. It wouldn't be helpful to rehash it here, but suffice it to say that 30 comments later, I wish I had simply said:

"You can feed your baby exclusively organic food, make sure their little hands never touch a piece of plastic and ensure their eyes don't take in a second of television, but if you're not raising them to be kind, considerate and thoughtful of others by your very example, I don't much care to know what you think about anything else. But, if you do happen to mess up, and you're mom enough to call yourself on it, I've got your back."

Growing greener an issue at a time

JUN 19

When it comes to saying I'm "green," I have to admit I feel like a total poser. I know I'm not alone in thinking that until I eat exclusively homemade, locally grown food, hand-stitch my own clothes out of organic hemp and drive a vehicle powered by biodiesel when motorized travel simply can't be avoided, I'm not really green enough to make much of a difference.

At least, that's what I used to think, until I started doing research for this column.*

Every time I asked people if they considered themselves "green," they paused, then ticked off a long list of what they could be doing better. Even people I've never seen swill from a plastic bottle or use a disposable diaper felt that because they could or should be doing more for the environment, they weren't doing enough.

That leads me to believe there are actually a lot of us green wannabes out there, and we need to start talking. After all, what you are doing right has an impact, regardless of the fact that there's room for improvement.

Ever since I turned over my own new leaf, environmentally speaking, I decided that when it comes to being green, variegated would be a perfectly acceptable shade for me.

The first commitment I made for the planet came under duress.

My 8-year-old brother watched my mom throw away one of those plastic six-pack holders that kill fish and seabirds. He'd just had an environmental impact lesson at school, and that prompted him to lecture us at length about how many fish and birds could die as a result of our carelessness.

My mom raised her eyebrows at me, then narrowed her eyes at him.

"This is what they're teaching you at school?" she said. "That I kill fish?"

She started muttering in Slovak as she continued wielding a meat cleaver.

My brother dropped the subject and backed out of the kitchen, but his admonition stuck with me. To this day, I can't toss one of those

---

* This was my first Confessions of a Green Wannabe column.

plastic yokes into the garbage without taking the scissors to it.

It's just one small thing, right? But I think that's how it works. We get turned on to new ideas, or better ways of doing things, and then incorporate what makes sense to us into our own lives.

At its core, I believe being green requires you to be willing to tell the truth about things—to be organic. For me, being organic is about being authentic and doing what you believe is right because you believe it's right, not because your neighbor does it or because your new boyfriend is into recycling or because your sister said so.

Being green isn't just about the actions you take to consciously care for the environment. It's about the reasons you are motivated to do so.

I'll be honest.

Do I want to do my part in making the environment healthier for my children and their children? Of course I do. But what really motivates me is money.

As a writer/stay-at-home mom, the more money I can save, the better. Once I acknowledge the truth of that without any twinge of guilt, shame or blame, I'm free to figure out how to combine my desire to save money with steps I can take to do my part toward living greener.

Being green isn't about pretending to be any certain way. It's about making sustainable choices that work for you and your family. It's about doing your part to take care of the environment without compromising your beliefs and what you know to be true about yourself.

I'm going to stop waiting until "later" when I'm more "ready to really do it right." I'm going to start here and now, with the view that being a green person comes down to the sum total of one's actions.

I believe it's true that small things done regularly add up to make a worthwhile difference. Being green isn't about the pursuit of perfection, rather the choice to continue working in that direction, one person and one issue at a time.

Turns out, toys aren't trivial at all

In 1983, there were riots over Cabbage Patch Kids. In 1996, there were stampedes over "Sesame Street's" Tickle Me Elmo. Back then, I couldn't understand these mothers going insane over something as trivial as toys.

Until last month, when I became that mother and came to realize it's not about the toy at all. In my defense, there was no actual physical aggression, but still, I did go a little overboard.

Evidently, the limits of my sanity were tested when shortly after bringing our baby home from the hospital, we decided it would be a good time to move. Contrary to what I once believed, having two kids isn't really twice as hard as just the one. However, moving with those same two kids, both under the age of three, turned out to be exponentially harder than any of our (numerous) previous moves.

After dragging the kids through house after house, getting our hopes up, and even making offers on three different properties, we wearily decided not to show our kids another one until we were sure it was going to be our next home. In my heart, I knew as soon as we saw The One that it was The One, but we waited until after the ink dried on all the paperwork before introducing it to the boys.

We were both excited to show our oldest our new house, for real this time. As we got to the top of the stairs, I heard my husband, without warning me, tell him that he could pick any room he wanted.

Our toddler recently discovered the movie "Cars" and instantly went for the room containing a toy truck based on Mater, one of the film's animated characters. No big deal. I figured I'd just grab another one of those trucks next time I was in town and have it waiting for him in the room I had originally chosen for him.

One small problem. I had no idea this particular toy was crazy expensive. It was $150 new. Yes, $150. For a toy truck. We were moving in a few days and I wanted that truck to be at the new house. But that's the thing: We just bought a new house on the promise that we would do a million things differently to cut our budget to make the new mortgage work - I mean near-exclusive use of cloth diapers, no store-bought salad dressing, and keeping our 25-inch television instead of buying the flat-screen that would look really good in our new house.

So, clearly, there is no room in the new budget for a $150 toy.

His dad said he'd forget all about it. Wrong. The kid's got an impressive, though suspiciously selective, memory.

He told people: "I move to new house. I get Mater truck." A few days before the big move, I searched eBay and found it for $50. While that wasn't in the budget either, it was more reasonable than the original price.

Still, it's a $50 toy and the thing doesn't even double as a vacuum. I engaged in a bidding war over it anyway until Matt reminded me there was plenty to love about our new house to help him get over the disappointment of not having the truck.

Lucky little guy—he didn't have to because our friend and real estate broker bought him the truck as a surprise.

Within a day of moving to the new house, our son started looking for the Mater truck. I told him he would have to be patient and help me unpack all the boxes until we found Mater. Had I known this was the key to getting us unpacked, I'd have paid full price in a heartbeat. Also, I would've waited another week before "finding" it.

When we opened the box, delivered to our door and addressed to him, his eyes lit up and he smiled with relief.

"Oh! There it is!"

When he's not busy finding things to tow with his buddy Mater, our son can be found collecting pine cones, worms and raspberries in our new backyard.

Practice self-preservation

As people throughout Yamhill County set about preserving jars of tomatoes, cucumbers and other treats from the garden, to be savored in the future, I'm thinking of preserving something else entirely. It's a form of self-preservation, if you will.

None of us knows when precisely we will draw our last breath.

For some, this is a morbid topic. But for me, it's a necessary one.

Once I had my first baby, the very thought of not seeing him through adulthood—and beyond—kept me awake at night. I had things I needed him to know, things he can't possibly understand now, but would be important later. So, I started a simple notebook of letters to him.

Several entries simply have the date at the top, followed by blank lines until another dated page appears a month or two later. That's life with a baby.

This busy time, revolving around the constant care of little guys, is the story of our life right now. And we're blessed to have it.

I take these notes so they'll know what it was like raising them, so they will have a piece of themselves preserved in these pages.

For the record, I have another little notebook, called a journal, which details some of the less delightful aspects of child rearing. But those aren't intended for future edification.

That's what makes this form of self-preservation different. It's for a very specific audience—the children. And I offer you no rules as to how to do it, only encouragement to simply start.

This idea of self-preservation isn't just for parents. It's for anyone who has a meaningful relationship with someone else and wishes to preserve some of their life story as a gift to them in the future.

If you feel at all moved to do so, please don't let details like less-than-perfect handwriting, notebook or method stop you from starting today.

You don't have to document anything as dramatic as your escape from behind the Iron Curtain, though I wish my parents would. A box of index cards featuring details of your ordinary life and random memories become significant to those you love when you aren't here anymore to tell them your stories.

What kids don't ask you about now, they will wonder about later.

I'm trying to persuade my husband to do this along with the rest of you. I'd love for him to write some notes to the kids about his days picking berries, driving tractors and swinging hammers, or about his first job, cleaning bricks to save up for a BMX bike.

It's knowing those stories that will help them understand the man that is their father.

If you're just not a notebook kind of person, start a file on your computer with each child's name on it. Add to it as you wish and print it out periodically.

If you're the crafty sort, consider using actual canning jars with small notes tucked inside.

Or, put a stack of index cards on a jump ring and write your favorite quotes or Bible verses on them. Here's the most important part – write why they matter to you.

I have two notebooks, one for each of my kids. I pretend I'll decorate them some day, but will probably hand them over in 20 years as plain as they are now.

The books are full of open letters to them about first milestones, with details of ordinary days and random memories. I write about why I ride them on manners; I write about what kind of men I hope they become; I write about my faith and what I hope they take from it as they form their own; I write about why I make the sign of the cross when I see an ambulance with its lights on, and why I tear up every time I hear our national anthem. I write about funny little things they say and do.

These are small, but significant things. The sum of these small things is who I am.

For now, they know me as the singer of favorite songs, reader of bedtime stories, sandwich maker, apple slicer, kisser of boo boos and toy picker-upper.

Someday, however, I would like them to know me as a person. Someday, I'd like to shed a little light on what mattered to me and perhaps most importantly, how deeply their very existence matters to me.

If by some unfortunate circumstance, I'm not able to do that in person, please direct them to the notebooks to the right of my desk.

Going meatless once a week

AUG 21

As a bona fide Eastern European, I am a fan of all things meat. The only thing I don't love about meat is cooking it.

When I started my gig as a stay-at-home mom, cooking something beyond a potluck side dish became part of my job description. I avoided the handling of raw meat whenever possible, but eventually had to go beyond ground turkey and frozen chicken breasts.

Then someone called me chicken for writing about change rather than living it. This reader suggested that if I really wanted to do something good for the planet, I should take a look at what I eat and consider going vegan—which is to say, not consume or use animal products of any kind.

Cutting all meat out of my life? And cheese? Not a chance. But more beans and fewer burgers? That I could do.

The reasons for going meatless are compelling—reducing the risk of chronic preventable conditions like cancer, cardiovascular disease, diabetes and obesity. This simple act can also help reduce your carbon footprint and save resources like fresh water and fossil fuel, according to the nonprofit initiative "Meatless Monday," in association with the Johns Hopkins Bloomberg School of Health.

I'm surprised the organization didn't mention the other major benefit—the fact that I wouldn't have to handle any more raw meat.

My meat-loving husband was a little nervous about all the vegetarian talk, despite the fact he had tried introducing me to tofu when we were dating. But we agreed to ease into the idea by reducing our portions of meat, replacing slabs of steak with strips, and increasing our intake of vegetables.

We also chopped meat off the menu once a week. We settled on what I so cleverly put in my planner as: "Meatless Mondays."

It turned out, of course, that I was not original with my alliteration. There is, in fact, an entire organization with that very name, committed to getting the word out with this simple slogan: "One day a week, cut out the meat."

For information about the Meatless Monday movement, more reasons to consider reducing your meat consumption, or recipes designed to make it all a little more palatable, visit www.meatlessmonday.com.

Since taking on the challenge of going vegetarian once a week, there have been failures, like the unfortunate incident of the smelly veggie patties. I stayed up until almost midnight the night before making them, and they weren't even edible.

Then there was my recent family fondue night brainstorm.

This might sound fun, but if your family includes a toddler and an infant, hold off on serving splattering hot cheese for consumption with sharp instruments. A smarter idea is to have a veggie pizza with garlic sauce delivered to your front door.

My new motto in the kitchen, admittedly not the makings for a hit cooking show, is, "How bad could it be?"

On the upside, I'm learning to appreciate tofu.

I still think it's mostly gross, and I apologize for that, but it is really not that bad after it absorbs other flavors. I know "not that bad" isn't a big sell, but the only other thing I've got is, "It's so good for you."

I've discovered a "Meatless Main Dishes" tab in some of my cookbooks. I had originally figured that was a euphemism for extra large portions of appetizer and salad.

Lentil soup sounded disgusting, but turned out to be delicious. My husband and 2-year-old both slurped up second helpings.

My husband thought, however, that the soup could be improved with the addition of ham. Smoked ham, specifically.

Maybe on Tuesday.

The keys for keeping kids safe at school

SEP 1

As the days grow shorter, and students and teachers begin dusting off backpacks and briefcases, I can't help but think of the news story dominating headlines before the final bell rang letting kids out for the summer. It was the story of Kyron Horman, the second-grader who vanished from the hallways of his elementary school in June, not to be seen or heard from since.[*]

Endless media coverage of the Horman story had parents giving the "stranger danger" talk sooner than anticipated.

Count me among them. As is my way, I overreacted initially, pulling all the blog posts relating to my kids and checking on them around the clock with the commitment of someone suffering from obsessive-compulsive disorder.

The more I thought about it, though, the more I realized it was ultimately worse for my children to be raised in an environment of fear and distrust. Fear, I decided, should not be allowed to win out here.

I did however, as you might have noticed, ask my editors to change the picture for this column to exclude my children—just in case. As I learned from a favorite uncle of mine, life is best lived with a balance of caution and courage.

While the Kyron Horman story has garnered national attention and put fear in the hearts of parents who previously assumed their children were safe on campus, little has been mentioned in the way of practical advice for helping you protect your child when you're not present.

So here, from the files of a former school secretary, are the keys for keeping kids safe at school: pay attention, plan ahead, put it in writing and partner with staff.

As soon as possible, make sure the school office has the correct contact information on record. Double-check the numbers for mobile phones, work phones and all of your emergency contacts.

Check that the list of people authorized to pick up your child is complete. And update this information periodically.

That's something I can't stress enough. I can't tell you how many

---

[*] And not found yet as of this writing.

times, during my school office days, when I was unable to contact parents or guardians because information was incomplete or incorrect.

Less urgent but still stressful were the many times someone came to pick up a child, but was not authorized to do so because we didn't have permission on the record in writing.

You need to know your school's policies and adhere to them. It might be irritating, but wouldn't you rather be a little late to the dentist than have someone take off with your kid without your knowledge or permission?

Putting it in writing and planning ahead go hand-in-hand when it comes to keeping kids safe. Last minute changes leave the door open for confusion and mistakes.

Emergencies happen. But unless your situation qualifies as one, avoid calling the school at the last minute to alter your child's after-school plans.

I'm quite certain that last-minute bus notes led to my hair starting to turn gray during my two-year grade school gig.

An article about keeping your kids safe at school wouldn't be complete without mentioning that the notion of a school nurse is a myth. Many schools don't have any medical professionals on campus at all, and certainly not the majority of the time.

Odds are, the person calling to report fevers, rashes or sprained ankles is the school secretary. And this school secretary received her medical training from Google.

Please learn the procedure for how medications are handled on campus and follow them as well. For the love of all that is holy, do not send your kid to school with a sandwich baggie full of aspirin.

You might be surprised to know that even cough drops have to be allocated from school offices.

I assure you, I would prefer kids be allowed to carry their own than come and see me. I'd rather not have to stop what I was doing, be it counting lunch money or applying a public school ice pack (water frozen in a Dixie cup), to unwrap a sticky Ricola.

If your child has serious allergies, make sure you supply the school with EpiPens and notices informing the school office, the classroom teacher and the cafeteria staff, in writing. Then follow up to make sure people are aware of your concern.

The key to doing this so that staff members don't cringe when they see you coming is simple: Be nice.

Understand that the system is run by human beings who are trying to manage moving targets. They are no more perfect than you, and they share your goal of seeing that your child is safe and successful in the school environment.

As your kids load up their backpacks before the first day of school, tuck a notepad into your glove box so you can write tardy and absence notes. And remember, the best way to fight the dark shadow of fear is to proceed with caution while still maintaining the courage to enjoy life.

You can go home again—sort of

On the leisurely walk home from our ninth anniversary dinner, my husband ruined everything. He had the audacity to suggest we take off next week on a family road trip.

"Not a chance," I responded to his eager request, killing both the idea and the good mood.

See, I'm a planner. None of this impromptu business for me, thank you very much. High on my list of reasons to justify my negative reaction was the fact that traveling with two children under the age of three sounded about as much fun as a bout of morning sickness.

A few days later, we got the news that a cherished member of our family had passed away. And we made arrangements to head north for his memorial service.

Since we were packing anyway, Matt brought up the vacation idea again. Fresh on my mind was the reality that life ends when you least expect it. So, we hit the road for a 10-day road trip.

It was like Jack Kerouac meets Humpty Dumpty, in the sense we traveled with no reservations, but with toddler tunes playing in the background. In retrospect, this turned out to be a journey through our roots.

To share at the memorial, we stocked up on the food of my people— sausage, sauerkraut and Slivovica, a type of plum brandy. And we visited my hometown, which consisted of sitting in traffic near the Tacoma Dome as I pointed out the church where I was baptized.

We stopped at Sea-Tac to pick up my dad, who flew 5,400 miles to pay his respects to one of his best friends. I don't get to see my parents much, now that they are back in Slovakia, so this part of the trip was a highlight.

We arrived at the hotel in time to meet my oldest friend for highballs, all eight of us toasting in one small room. Just like old times, only we were the ones in charge of making sure everyone got meals, naps and baths.

Somewhere in the middle of that sleepless night, I decided this family trip was a terrible idea after all. Never again, I vowed.

The next morning, we had a family reunion of sorts while

celebrating Ujo Relo.

Matt stayed at the hotel with the kids, and still managed to make an awesome kapustnica (sauerkraut soup, for the uninitiated) in the Crock-Pot. Never mind that we could smell it from the elevator.

After parting ways with my family, we headed to the dock to catch the ferry for Bremerton, where we planned to visit my college roommate. We arrived just in time to wave as the ferry pulled out.

It would be more than an hour until the next one embarked for Bremerton. So Matt took Sam for a walk.

In the rear-view mirror I saw this Norman Rockwellian image of a little boy with chocolate ice cream on his face, waving an American flag in one hand and holding his dad's hand with the other. Maybe we should do more of this, I thought.

The sweet image stayed with me until we settled into our campsite near Puget Sound and discovered our mattress pump didn't work.

While Matt might be considered a hardcore camper to some—OK, to me—what with that "no room for pillows, just roll up your sweatshirt" nonsense, he did his best to make sure we were comfortable. He even went so far as to blow it up, using the exhaust pipe of our car.

Pillows or no, I love that guy. We should definitely do this more often.

We continued north to Bellingham.

I had left my college town a full decade ago, in the Geo Metro with the mismatched doors and reddish hood, spray-painted by Gypsies, the strains of Pink Floyd blaring from the cassette deck. I had headed south to visit my boyfriend in McMinnville. I returned this time with the same guy—the one I now call my husband—but in a professionally painted minivan with Thomas the Tank Engine playing on the DVD.

When we drove into the town where we first became an "us," we felt a temptation to visit our favorite spots and roam around campus. But during a loop through the neighborhood where we used to live, both kids fell asleep, and we decided to keep on rolling. In truth, we were tourists now. We couldn't go back and visit what we wanted to because it no longer exists. The old us had faded into fond memories and evidence of our new life was sleeping peacefully in car seats.

We wrapped up our trip in Walla Walla, where we had an impromptu reunion with Matt's family. We woke up that morning with both boys in our bed, everyone tangled together, still sleepy but clean and happy.

The memory of that cozy scene is what led me to agree to Matt's next brainstorm, purchase of a dedicated camping van. I named her "Wanda."

Captain of the kitchen keeps her cuisine lean

OCT 16

How I passed home economics in middle school is a mystery to me. I wonder about this between Google searches for "uses for stale bread" and "can you roast butternut squash seeds?"

Stale bread and squash seeds are just some of the many items I'd have simply tossed in the trash in my pre care-about-the-Earth, need-to-save-money days. But no longer.

During my childhood, my mom lost more than a little sleep wondering how I was going to make it as an adult in this world, what with my willful ignorance regarding all things domestic. Her frequent, frustrated refrain was: "Necessity will teach you!"

Oh, and has it ever. And school has been in session in a particularly big way since I became a mom myself.

When my oldest son was born three years ago, saving money became my way of earning it. So I was forced to come up with a few home ec hacks of my own.

But what, you might wonder, does this have to do with being eco-conscious?

Everything. If you take a holistic approach to being green, that is.

Consider for a moment that the root word "eco" comes from the Greek word for "house." To have a solid house, you need to take care of your finances as well as your environment. Economics as well as ecology.

If you look at being eco-conscious from that perspective, it makes sense that taking a look at your personal economics is another opportunity to live "greener."

While I've seldom been accused of wearing rose-colored glasses, I find myself wondering if there isn't a bright side to this collective economic disruption. I know I'm not alone in needing to find a silver lining somewhere, to stave off depression from reading, hearing and talking about all the different ways the sky is falling.

So, is it really falling? Or are we just approaching an inevitable crossroads, forcing us to choose which direction we want to go as individuals and a society? Is it really such a bad thing to come to terms with who you really are and who you really want to be?

For my money, what there is of it, we have an opportunity—a responsibility, even—to navigate ourselves out of this economic mess in a way that is sustainable for future generations. This means making changes in the way we do things—real changes, people.

When I say "real changes," I don't mean major, costly, life-altering changes. I just mean tweaking your habits.

I started with the way I go about the care and feeding of my family. Here are a few things I've learned to help save the Earth, and some dough, while putting bread on the table: Learn the art of cupboard cooking. Essentially, this means learning to use what you have on hand, avoiding extra trips to the store. Eventually you'll get to where you score sweet deals on sale items because you know what you use, what you have and what you need. For fun, work with your partner and/or children to see who can come up with the tastiest cupboard concoctions.

Create a consistent theme night schedule to simplify meal planning and preparation. For example, Meatless Monday, Taco Tuesday, Wok Wednesday and so forth.

Instead of trying to develop an actual menu, try having key ingredients on hand to build any number of quick meals—breakfast fare, soups and salads, stir fry staples and the like. Plan for leftovers and be creative with them. One mid-week night we plan on leftovers, but use the Hungarian term "maradeky." That sounds so much fancier than "random contents found while cleaning out the fridge."

Do yourself a favor and prep cook early in the week. Chop a few onions, peel some carrots, shred some cheese and so forth. For fun, invite a friend over to share the chores and split the rewards. Make your own frozen mixed-veggie packs by cleaning, chopping and freezing your favorites and sealing them in a freezer-proof bag for later use.

Make your own convenience foods. Look at the ingredients on the packaged foods you buy at the store and see what it would take to re-create them at home. I'm not that clever, actually. I just Google it. I'm still on a mission, though, to learn the best way to make granola bars, veggie patties and fruit rollups.

Meet your new food storage system, consisting of masking tape, a Sharpie and some recycled food containers. You won't see them featured in any of Martha Stewart's magazines but it works. Better labeling leads to less waste.

Bottle or breast? Yes!

NOV 3

When it comes to how to feed your baby, word on the street is, "Breast is best."

I assumed, like many new mothers do, that because nursing was natural, it would also be easy. But it wasn't.

Rewarding? Yes. Easy? No.

In the beginning, I exposed myself to half of Yamhill County as I struggled to strike a natural nursing pose with my voracious firstborn. I felt self-conscious in public, particularly when it was clear I was making other people uncomfortable.

The American Academy of Pediatrics recommends mothers nurse exclusively for the first six months, and, after introducing solid foods, to the baby's first birthday and beyond, as long as mutually desired.

From my experience, however, the general public seemed insistent on me breastfeeding initially—"You are going to breast feed, aren't you?"—then increasingly put off as baby began to age—"You're still nursing him?"

Sam weaned himself at 16 months. Jake, on the other hand, didn't get the AAP memo and abruptly stopped at nine months. To make it clear he didn't desire my continued attempts to feed him, he started biting every time I tried.

While things went smoothly with Sam, I had nothing but compassion for friends who felt judged by family, strangers and the medical community for formula-feeding their babies. But it wasn't until I found myself up in the middle of the night, unable to meet Jake's most basic need, that I really understood the inadvertent damage done by me and the rest of the breastfeeding lobby.

In an effort to raise awareness about the benefits of breastfeeding, I'm afraid we've created a breeding ground for judgment and guilt when mothers turn to formula to feed their babies—a culture of hostility, if you will. We happen to live in a particularly pro-breastfeeding part of the country. Portland was rated fifth among best cities for babies by Parents magazine, citied specifically for the area's positive breastfeeding accommodations and attitudes.

That's awesome, really, if you're one of those breastfeeding moms. It's not so awesome for mothers who can't nurse, or choose not to, and feed their babies by bottle instead of breast.

There are a host of reasons for mothers to use formula. Not once, however, have I heard someone say they use formula for lack of caring.

Hopefully, that sounds absurdly obvious to most readers. But there is an attitude around formula feeding that implies the mother didn't try or didn't care enough.

I know, because I got smacked in the face with it during a recent all-night bout with Google, trying to troubleshoot how to keep my baby nursing when he's decided to quit at nine months.

No amount of herbs or Mother's Milk tea was going to fix what this little guy needed—a full belly. So I got some formula.

What I wish I could tell you is that it was as easy as realizing what he needed and setting about getting it. But it wasn't.

I was wracked with guilt.

At first I considered suing the La Leche League for emotional damages.* Then I started talking to mothers on both sides of this debate, and I discovered we were doing this to each other. It's the looks. The comments. The assumptions. The smugness. Enough already.

I understand the reasoning behind the "breast is best" campaign. I'm thankful for having been able to do it myself and glad I got so much support.

But I also believe formula is a fine, nutritional alternative. Honestly, to hear some people talk, you'd think I was tossing my kid a crack pipe.

I think the sum of our choices affects the health and well-being of our children more than our answer to this one question—"bottle or breast?" I think a mother should be allowed to feed her baby from the breast or the bottle without feeling judged or condemned by the self-righteous who haven't walked in her shoes.

For the record, I'm rabidly pro-choice. And by that I mean, I respect your choice even if it's not the same as mine. As for me and my kids, the answer to the bottle or breast question is, "Yes!"

---

*   You guys know I'm kidding, right? You can't be this far into the book and not know
      that about me by now but in case you opened to this page and saw that I figured I'd
      mention that it was a joke. I'm a humor-in-hard-places person, obviously. I am a fan
      of the La Leche League and admire what the organization has done for many
      mamas and their littles. I am, however, not at all a fan of hatey people who hurt
      others with their judgey, mean words and actions.

Adventures in toilet training

DEC 1

All I want for Christmas is for my three-year-old to wake up able to use the bathroom without help, without making a mess with the toilet paper, and, most importantly, without causing any more stress for either one of us.

Sometimes being a parent feels like a live version of the childhood game, "What's grosser than gross?"

I thought being covered in an avalanche of baby vomit was the most disgusting thing that ever happened to me. But that was before we started our adventures in potty training.[*]

Remember the children's television segment, "One of these things is not like the others?" That's how potty training is going at our house. All the tricks people swear by are failing to work. Worse, many seem to be backfiring.

I tried the "heap on the praise" approach. The first time my son peed in the toilet I made such a big fuss over it he looked at me like I'd lost my mind.[**]

If I walked in on you in the bathroom and clapped and cheered, how would you react? There's your visual on how Sam responded to that technique.

I adore reading to my children, except when it comes to insipid potty-themed books. Those I've come to hate.

While I've heard they work well with most kids, mine picks up hidden take-home messages. For example, Sam was infatuated with "Once Upon a Potty," a book about a little boy named Joshua and his uber-patient mother.

Sam insisted on using the bathroom "like Joshua" before his nap.

For Sam, that meant: "He sat and sat and sat and then nothing happened." So I left him in the bathroom to wait some more. Big mistake.

The entire roll of toilet paper ended up in the bowl. Luckily, nothing had happened.

---

[*]   Oh, Fun Fact: It's called toilet learning now.
[**]   Matt would like the record to reflect he didn't have all the information about what went into the toilet before determining the route we went to fix it. I added this story to the list of things we'll laugh about someday.

I decided to wait until he mastered the basics before discussing the all-important issue of which direction to hang the toilet paper. Right now, as far as Sam is concerned, it all unravels the same.

I even tried using candy as a reward. For a kid who never eats candy, this was a big deal. And it worked, until Sam started gaming the system.

When I told him he couldn't have a piece of candy for holding his pee and going a tablespoon at a time, he had another fit. I finished off the M&Ms while giving myself a time-out in the pantry.

Then there's the Cheerio trick. Apparently I didn't explain it well enough, because Sam got the impression we were throwing all of his baby brother's food into the toilet.

I explained the intended Cheerio-as-target concept to him as I fished out the glass jar of carrots. What I didn't know was that he'd tossed the lid in, too, knocking the toilet out of commission.

So far, potty training has been costly.

We spent I don't know how much on Thomas the Tank Engine underwear, M&Ms and disinfecting wipes. That's not to mention $175 for a new toilet and $500 to have it installed.

Then there was my sanity.

I'd love nothing more than to end this article by telling you that it was all worth the dramatic cost, because Sam now uses the bathroom happily and independently. But that's not our story.

I thought he was ready. He was curious, so he seemed ready.

But he wasn't, no matter what his grandparents think or Joshua's mom has to say.

While it's good to pay attention to developmental guidelines, in order to flag potential problems, it seems the parents who enjoy their children the most are the ones who learn to go with the flow—even when the thing that's flowing requires immediate cleanup. For now, going with the flow means declaring a hiatus on all toilet talk until Sam is ready, because, as his dad so succinctly put it, the kid has the winning hand on this one.

Maybe Santa will come through with my Christmas miracle. Maybe not.

Either way, may he tuck a little extra patience into my stocking for our next adventure.

A list of 'ecolutions' for 2011

DEC 18

I'll be honest with you. There are days I wish I'd never gone public with my desire to create a greener life.

As a wannabe, I always had good intentions and a long list of excuses for not living up to them. But since going public with my confession, I'm finding integrity getting in the way of convenience.

There seems to be so much more I could or should be doing on the environmental front. Sometimes it gets so overwhelming, I want to throw in my organic bamboo towel.

If I had one, maybe I would. But I'm still using towels inherited from my childhood home.

Now that I think of it, that's green living right there. But still ... Yoo-hoo. Santa?

As I reflect on the past year, and look toward the new one, I'm happy to share this: Despite some misgivings, I've become a greener person since starting this column. Some of the ways I've changed have become so much a part of my new "normal," in fact, that I had to really think about what we do now that's different.

For many of us, New Year's resolutions are a perpetual list of guilt and shame. I implore you to stop this mental madness and instead turn this traditional time of reflecting on the past year into an opportunity to celebrate what you have accomplished and to create more of what you want in the upcoming year.

Remember, it begins next month. So don't go all crazy.

Start with a specific goal, followed with a clear plan of action. Otherwise, you just have the makings of an adult's letter to Santa.

Instead of "save the whales," you might try something like, "take shorter showers." Then you need to adopt an action plan to accomplish that.

Since I have two little guys at home, I don't exactly linger over my loofah. So I chose some other green goals for new year.

My list of ecolutions might read like a remedial home economics syllabus, but I'm a stay-at-home mom who believes we can make the most significant difference by starting where we are with the resources we have. Here are some of the things I've done differently in the past year, or are looking forward to trying in the new one:

Tweaking my work habits to reduce my professional carbon footprint. I'm editing more on the computer, cutting back on what I print, recycling everything I can and quitting my habit of buying and hoarding office supplies.

Using cloth napkins for meals and dishrags for cleaning up. I had no idea a roll of paper towels could last so long.

Giving less material gifts and using creative, greener wrapping ideas like reusing brown bags with old ornaments attached and paint chips as gift tags. Or, for baby showers, wrapping gifts with receiving blankets. This year I'd like to learn to use my sewing machine to make more gifts.

Keeping cloth shopping bags tucked into the stroller and trunk of my car. I just need to remember to bring them into the store with me.

Cutting down on waste and trips to the grocery store by learning how to cook out of the cupboards and figuring out a meal-planning method that works for us.

Washing clothes exclusively in cold water, reserving warm for diapers, sheets and towels. Next year, I'd like to be more diligent about using the clothesline.

Unplugging appliances and chargers and shutting down the computer overnight. This has become such a habit my fingers itch to pull the plug when visiting friends.

Springing for greener cleaners. Next year I'd like to learn to make my own.

Reducing the amount of packaging we send to the landfill by making my own baby food, bread and bread crumbs. Next, I'd like to figure out how to make soup stock and granola bars.

I know that sounds random, but we use a lot of both and they can't be that hard to make.

I want to grow some of our own food next year, as well as get over my irrational fear of composting. This one has been on my perpetual ecolution list, so I make no promises.

Happy New Year!

More friends aren't more work

JAN 5

Turning down the opportunity to make more friends is like saying "I already have enough money; you can keep my lottery winnings." Who does that?

Well, I do. Or, rather, I did when my obstetrician suggested I look into joining a local moms group. I told him: "I'm not really in the market for new friends."

I know that makes me sound like a jerk. What I was trying to say was that I was already overwhelmed. Since I wasn't able to make time to meet with my current friends, how could I possibly make new ones?

Making mom friends is not unlike forming any other friendship. Basically, it's always like the first day of a new school, when you walk to the cafeteria, heart in your stomach, hoping you have a cool enough lunch, and that, please God, people will invite you, or at least allow you, to sit at their table.

There are, however, a few unique traits to a new mom friendship. You can almost count on exchanging intimate details of fertility issues, labor and delivery. Then you might move on to sharing highlights from nursing (or not) traumas and commiserating over the military-grade sleep deprivation torture that is having a newborn baby.

Depending on the ages of your children, you will move on to potty training, now called potty learning, to the debate over vaccination and whether or not you plan to have more children.

It is very likely for all of this to take place prior to exchanging first names. Also, you might be having this conversation somewhere as intimate as the checkout line at Fred Meyer.

As it did in middle school, lunch bag contents still matter. Instead of hoping your lunch is cool enough, though, you might be concerned with whether or not your kids' snacks are healthy enough.

If you've been pregnant for more than 10 minutes, you've likely already learned that parenting today is a competitive sport.

So, as you give your kids a muffin, you sort of want to assure the other moms within earshot that it's homemade, with mostly organic ingredients. But then, you know, you don't want to sound too, well, like "that" mom. It will never be really clear what that means exactly, you'll just be certain you don't want to seem like "that."

It's tricky navigating the course of any new friendship. But it's worth the effort to have a few understanding friends in your speed dial* so that when you feel like putting the baby on the front porch until help arrives, you know someone's one the way with cocktails and Kleenex.

The truth about being a stay-at-home mom is that it's not exactly a self-esteem builder. Whatever you did or didn't accomplish before having children doesn't apply here.

My children aren't so much concerned with my personal interests as they are curious about the particles of food I missed with the vacuum. And that's fine, because it's their job to be kids. It's on me to find a way to be a nurturing mother to them 24-7, without wanting to stick my head in the oven.

That sounds harsh, I know. Unless you have, or have been around, a teething baby and a toddler intent on "why-ing" you to death.

A good friend will hold you up, not tear you down or judge you for falling. So where do you find these good friends when simply running back-to-back errands with your well-behaved darlings wipes you out?

It turns out my obstetrician had the right idea when I waddled out of his office nearly four years ago: Try a moms group.

I finally checked one out a few weeks ago, and I'm already breathing differently. Literally. Another mom in the group suggested a breathing technique to try when that rage that no one talks about bubbles to the surface. To my utter amazement, it worked wonders. There are some differences among the women in this group but we all love our children and want to do our best by them. I figure that's as great a common ground as any.

Even though I'm blessed to have several amazing girlfriends, I've learned that in the life of a mom with young children, there's always room for more friends who can talk through the din of playing children, can empathize with the dementia that comes with day-long diapering, and share your need to talk incessantly about seemingly insignificant details.

It's also wonderful to be able to hang out with people who speak in full—albeit interrupted—sentences, and who enjoy being in the company of people who might just be as tired as you are.

Not, of course, that it's a contest.

---

* Speed dial used to be a thing. Now it's kind of all pretty speedy, compared to say rotary phones which I used to call my first crush and can now be found at your local antique store.

Kitchen interest comes full circle

FEB 2

Let me preface this by saying, I'm no expert on nutrition. Despite the fact I was raised by a physician father and chef mother, the latter dishing up gourmet meals as a matter of course, I left home a bulimic with no clue how to properly feed herself.

Throughout my college years, I ate a steady diet of pizza, dormitory-grade turkey tetrazzini and Sourdough Jacks. I thought adding hot dogs to my Kraft macaroni and cheese was really kicking it up a notch.

Flash forward 15 years, and I'm raising two kids who consume tofu, avocados and black beans as finger food, and dig their greens to the point of asking for seconds.

It's not that I've never handed a french fry over the back seat. But as someone with an eating-disordered brain, it was important for me to start my kids on a healthier path right from the beginning.

Believe me, if I can learn how to make nutrition a priority, anyone can. Here are a few of the things that worked for me:

First of all, I am conscious of not creating a power struggle around food. I see it like this: It's my son's body, but it's my job to teach him how to take the best possible care of it.

I try to relate nutrition to Sam's interests. And he loves cars so much, he works them into mealtime metaphors.

He told me the other night that my soup tasted like it came from the junkyard. I told him he needed to continue fueling his body.

I give the boys as many choices as possible, while making the things that matter most to me non-negotiable.

Does he want the blue bowl or the green one? Does he want his sauce on the meat or beside it? I'm fine either way.

But not trying a bite? Not an option.

If he doesn't like it, as was the case with the junkyard soup, he doesn't have to finish it. But he does have to take one fully chewed and swallowed bite.

Presentation, I've learned, matters.

One of my favorite healthy eating concoctions is the muffin meal. I fill five of the six cups in a muffin pan with an assortment of finger food. If Sam eats everything in the cups, he gets a little dessert in the sixth one.

Speaking of dessert, I've found that adding the words "cake" and "surprise" to the names of dishes that might otherwise get snubbed works wonders. This re-naming strategy is one of my most effective mama tools.

Sam won't touch "green sauce," but he asks for extra "verde sauce."

Finally, if all else fails, break out the blender. For a long time, when Sam got it in his head that something was gross—even though he liked it two days ago—I would clear his plate, dump the contents in a blender, add yogurt, top it with sprinkles and serve it with a fancy spoon.

This worked beautifully until Sam recognized a piece of his dinner in his parfait one night. Then the jig was up.

Since I started cooking with my wanna-be-helpful but messy 3-year-old, I have more insight as to how crazy I must have driven my own mom in the kitchen.

It's not that she didn't try to teach me to cook. I just wasn't into it.

During my teen years, my mom and I didn't have a lot of patience with each other. And something about the kitchen made it an emotional pressure cooker.

Since my kid isn't rolling his eyes at me and muttering under his breath—at least not yet—I love cooking with him. I think it encourages him to try new things when he's invested in the process.

As for my mom and me, these days she's teaching me to cook through cross-continental e-mails, because I want to know how she made her Kapustnica. I'm thankful for the second chance to learn from my mom.

I'm even keeping her three-page instructions for her "easy" strudel tucked into my recipe box. But perhaps she's more confident in my cooking abilities than I am, because I keep looking for my truly easy granola recipe instead.

There's room for many ways of parenting

MAR 2

When The Wall Street Journal ran an article headlined, "Why Chinese Mothers are Superior," it triggered a new round of "Mommy wars." It launched a vicious debate on the merits and methods of Chinese parenting in comparison to its Western counterpart.

However, that missed the entire point of Amy Chua's essay, which was excerpted from her recently published memoir, "Battle Hymn of the Tiger Mother."

For starters, the headline didn't accurately reflect the spirit of Chua's work. The Yale professor didn't intend her memoir to serve as a "how to" parenting manual, nor as a modern day "Mommie Dearest."

Tiger Mama-style parenting doesn't require wire hangers. It just requires banishing fear of a child's failure in favor of faith in her ability to succeed.

While many parts of the article gave me pause, it featured one line that might actually change how I parent my boys:

"Western parents are extremely anxious about their children's self-esteem. They worry about how their children will feel if they fail at something. Western parents are concerned about their children's psyches.

"Chinese parents aren't. They assume strength, not fragility."

I, like Chua, am a first-generation American. My parents were fond of reminding me a family was not a democracy.

They wanted nothing to do with all that self-esteem business. They figured self-esteem wasn't something you got; it was something you earned.

Reading Chua's words made me realize, for the first time, where my parents were coming from. Here, this whole time, they'd just assumed I was strong and capable.

But actually having a heart-to-heart about our feelings wasn't exactly how they did things. I was just supposed to realize that, and now I do.

Not everyone feels the love for Chua. Since the publication of her book in January, she has received a steady stream of criticism, leading up to and including death threats.

Death threats? Seriously? Come on, people. Defensive much?

Why is it that we are collectively so afraid to tell the truth about how hard it can be to be a parent? And why is it so hard to allow for people to parent differently without feeling like it's a commentary on what we do or don't do ourselves?

How about we quit pretending there is only one right way to raise children and agree to stop fighting about what that mythical "best" way is? Instead, let's use that energy to learn from one another's methods and mistakes.

Remember this: You are the expert on your children. Parenting is personal. But that doesn't mean you have to take everything personally.

I think Chua should be applauded for her courage.

That's not because I agree with every single thing she did. Not even Chua claims that.

It's because she stands by the spirit in which she mothered—fiercely, believing in her kids the best way she knew how, and never, ever giving up on them, even when it meant looking into her own heart to re-examine her role as a mother and how to best meet her daughters' needs. That is something to be proud of.

Chua's controversial memoir speaks to our potential as parents. If we take nothing else from her experience, consider this: It takes enormous courage to be honest about parenting and great strength to stay the course in the face of criticism.

Perhaps most importantly, it takes a goodly measure of grace to admit possible error and embrace a different approach. To recognize our imperfection from the outset, but pledge to do our best each and every day anyway, is the most genuine statement we can make about parenting.

Taking a leaf from the nanny

APR 6

I'll let you in on a favorite parenting secret of mine. Sometimes, particularly out in public, I pretend I'm the nanny.

This comes in handy when my toddler nearly dives into the water feature at Wilco, or takes it upon himself to "deadhead" the flower display as I wrestle my 1-year-old charge into the shopping cart. When people shoot me the stink eye, I just shake my head along with them, nanny-like.

The nanny thing works at home as well.

The way I see it, nannies actually have fun with their darling charges because they aren't as emotionally attached to the outcome. They don't worry so much about messes and are far more playful.

I know, because I worked as a nanny all through school.

Of course, that was back when I thought having kids was an exclusive fun-fest. I wondered what all the fuss and stress were about.

I laugh now as I recall being surprised when my employer would have me over even when she was home, saying she needed to "actually finish something." Now I get it.

By this time of year, most stay-at-home parents have tapped their reservoir of ideas for indoor fun. Parents and children alike are done with the fort-building, sick of play dough and over watching "Cars" on TV.

Since we have an entire season of schizophrenic spring weather to endure before summer comes along, make like the nanny and have some fun with it.

Moms worry that wet feet cause colds. Nannies get rain boots and take kids out for puddle stomps. Nannies gear up and get as wet as their charges.

Yes, you will get wet. You might even get muddy. But you might surprise yourself by having at least as much fun as your kids.

For more fun ideas, check out Rebecca P. Cohen's "15 Minutes Outside: 365 Ways to Get Out of the House and Connect with Your Kids," or visit her website at http://www.rebeccaplants.com.

Back inside, try re-purposing old toys in new ways. I took Sam's tool bench and turned it into a library station, for example.

You can make personalized library cards. Or, if you're a hack like me, you can dig a few rewards cards out of your wallet, put a strip of masking tape on them and write kids' names on them with a marker.

Note: Don't use your credit card, because these young patrons lose library cards in less time than it takes you to fashion a replacement.

For us, the key to this game is the "zoop, zoop" machine. It means being willing to approximate that sound each time a book is checked out.

When library play gets old, try combining shaving cream and food coloring to make a new painting medium. Any time you do something out of the ordinary, and are able to sit down and get your hands dirty alongside them, kids love it.

As much as your patience allows, include your kids in your chores and favorite activities—cooking, gardening, yoga or whatever. It doesn't matter what you do so much as that you're engaged with them as you're doing it.

Sure, it's messier. And it takes longer. But that's all part of the job.

When we spend some quality time together early in the day, I find it leads to a less chaotic "fend for yourselves" playtime in the afternoon.

The kids seem okay with playing quietly when they've had fun with me earlier. I also feel zero guilt popping in an episode of "Bob the Builder" while I make dinner.

Obviously, the benefit of being the nanny is getting to clock out at the end of the day. But even on the days I want to lock myself in the bathroom and slam a few highballs, by the time those babies are in bed, sleeping peacefully, I am beyond grateful that I get to keep them.

Unplugged interval inspires soul-searching

APR 23

Readers of this column know by now that when it comes to individual efforts to save the planet, I'm an advocate for small things adding up as well as taking a tangential approach to what it means to be responsible stewards of our environment.

I think taking good care of our mental environment directly correlates to our ability, and interest, in caring for our physical one. This is why I can connect my experience with being forcibly "unplugged" to the popular Earth Day campaigns urging people to do the same.

Of course, the Earth Day campaigns suggest people simply unplug their electronics for a day or week.

I decided not to take that particular challenge because, like giving up sugar for Lent, it would be impossible for me. Then, two days before my 35th birthday, I dumped a 12-ounce mocha all over my computer and watched it crash before my tearful eyes.

"Hey, I thought of what you could get me for my birthday!" I told my husband. The gift, I thought, would be the new computer.

Instead, it was an unexpected examination of my time and a revelation of how I was spending it—which brings me to the concept of "phantom power."

As the environmental movement went mainstream, unplugging electronics while not in use was lauded as one small thing everyone could do to help the cause.

Lately, the perception seems to be that simply unplugging is too small an action to matter, so why bother? To that I say it's just a start.

Because there is more to do doesn't mean little steps don't matter. There are a lot of people who still leave all their appliances turned on, or plugged in, when they aren't using them, even overnight.

According to environmental writer Collin Dunn, phantom energy "sucks extra energy from the grid into your home when you aren't looking and you don't need it."

Well, folks, that's exactly what was happening to me. Whereas I thought the Internet was a helpful tool, it was draining my energy without my even knowing it.

While I stand by my earlier assertion that social media sites serve as a virtual water cooler for stay-at-home parents, once I stopped checking in at said water cooler, initially under duress, it changed my life for the better.

It's not that I was on the computer all day long, incessantly updating my Facebook status and ignoring my kids. But the way I was using e-mail, social media and Google had quite honestly become a replacement for how I used to use food and cigarettes. Any time I wasn't quite sure what to do next with my kids, or I'd made it through a tough transition, or I'd settled an argument over who got to play with the Mater truck, I rewarded myself with a "quick" break online.

I literally itched my way through the first day without Internet. I didn't quite have to join Facebook Anonymous, but I did have to recognize I had a problem, come to terms with it, overcome a sense of shame about wasting so much time without even knowing it and adjust to a new way of doing things.

As a result, where my days once felt fractured, they now feel focused. Where I felt frazzled, I now feel calm. Where there was never enough time, it has expanded to fill the gap. It's been a disorienting but wonderful experience.

Of course, it wasn't just the absence of engaging in old habits that changed things for me. It was also doing things in a new way.

During my forced hiatus, instead of firing up my Google machine, I called my mom for her meat loaf recipe and her advice on how to store ginger. I used my cookbooks for easy recipes with ingredients I was more likely to have on hand than the Internet ones I couldn't even pronounce. Instead of trying to look up ideas for creative things to do with my kids, I just did them.

If you have already unplugged for Earth Day, as many campaigns have urged, good for you.

If you haven't, consider taking a break from your electronics long enough to consider how your habits impact both your mental and physical environment. At the very least, move your coffee away from your computer.

By the way, you can still "friend" me on Facebook at Nathalie's Notes, I just might not get back to you right away.

Fasten your seat belt, mom; it will be a ride to remember

MAY 4

Before any airplane lifts off, passengers hear a safety spiel instructing them to secure their own oxygen mask before assisting others. When I climbed on the merry-go-round of motherhood, applying the oxygen mask theory could have prevented a three-year build up to my personal May Day meltdown.

I'll spare you the therapist's transcript and just say that equating being a good mother with putting your family's needs above all others, including your own, can lead to a crash landing.

Tending a newborn and toddler at the same time, and simultaneously juggling a move to a new place in a new town while going without sleep, it was hard for me to tell whether I was simply reaching a personal breaking point or something more serious was afoot. All I knew for sure is this: While I loved being a mom, I felt myself becoming a shell of who I used to be.

Perhaps the most frustrating thing was the assumption by others that I was in control of my time because I wasn't holding down a job outside the home. This was actually the farthest thing from reality.

I felt I was failing at a job that was supposed to come naturally. My deepest fear was not being competent enough to be a good mother, and every misstep seemed to confirm it.

Being puked, pooped and peed on as a routine part of the job isn't exactly an esteem-builder.

Then there's the underlying fundamental that everything you do in taking caring of a family gets undone in equal and opposite reaction.

Dirty laundry begins to pile up before the last load is folded. Dishes in the sink are a constant. And meals get eaten in a fraction of the time it takes to prepare them—assuming they don't wind up on the freshly mopped floor.

Around here, when my husband asks how I'm doing, I say I'm planning to stick my head in the oven as soon as I get a few minutes to pre-heat it. He laughs and reminds me we don't have a gas oven.

While a sense of humor helps, the truth is, there's nothing funny about depression.

When my doctor suggested I seek help, I agreed. I started figuring out the logistics of getting to the appointment, and before I knew it, I was experiencing chest pain and breathing difficulty.

Instead of calling 911, I turned to Google (though neither the *News-Register* nor I endorse this as a safe and sane practice). Google said, and my therapist eventually concurred, that my anxiety had reached a level beyond the "normal" range.

This was serious enough to catch my attention. It forced me to reconsider my previous assumption that it was selfish of me to make meeting my own needs a priority.

It occurred to me that instead of waiting hopefully for someone to give me chunks of time all to myself, I had to simply take them. Without identifying and voicing my needs, how could anyone help me?

When I put myself at the top of my list instead of the bottom, time somehow expanded to allow me to do the things that needed to be done without worrying so much about what didn't. A series of small things, like working out alone, breaking projects into micro-movements so I could make steady progress and learning to embrace instead of fight the chaos that comes with having small children all helped me repair my eroded self-esteem.

I know these aren't the sweet sentiments expected to come with a parenting column printed around Mother's Day, but I think truly honoring motherhood requires talking honestly about the entire journey, not just the Kodak moments.

All mothers deserve to be absolved from the myth of perfection. All mothers deserve the gift of time to themselves, and not just a few hours a year, but on a regular basis.

Not all of us know that we're the ones in charge of making sure that happens. Mamas, for Mother's Day this year, treat yourself to the gifts you extend to others daily—patience, forgiveness and understanding.

After a few years of navigating the thrills, twists and turns of being a new mom, I have this advice for expectant parents: Fasten your seatbelts. Remember that turbulence is temporary. Secure your own oxygen mask before assisting others. And, of course, enjoy the ride.

Permission to practice parenting

When I signed up for the Love and Logic parenting class at my son's school, I thought it was going to be the answer to my prayers.

The cover of the manual read: "Early Childhood Parenting Made Fun! Creating Happy Families and Responsible Kids From Birth to Six."

Finally! Just what I'd been waiting for!

Then, in smaller print down below, came the catch. It was a workbook, not a magic manual. Instead of getting all the answers, it offered something even better: permission to practice at parenting.

Like your children, I'm sure, my boys are angels most of the time. But there are those moments when they turn on me, leaving me wondering what possesses them.

In this group of parents searching for effective ways to relate to, and raise, their children, it was nice to discover I wasn't the only one ever bitten by her darling-turned-demon.

More times than I care to admit, I've pretended not to see something because I had no clue how to handle it. Or, worse, I've reacted to misbehavior without giving myself time to respond appropriately.

This class, taught by the lovely Jennifer Bass, gave me strategies for what to do when I didn't know what to do, which is much of the time when you have two toddlers.

Two key elements in this parenting philosophy are having a sense of humor and genuine empathy for children.

One of the class exercises was to come up with our own "empathetic statement" to use before delivering a consequence. Suggestions included: "bummer", "this is so sad," and "bless your heart."

We were instructed to write our selected statement on a sticky note as a reminder to use them. I passed my husband a note in class with my suggested phrase: "You better run!"

Joking aside, I quickly added the phrase, "This is so sad!" to my arsenal. I eliminated the following: "I'm serious," "I mean it," and "One, two, two and a half, three," because I learned the danger of getting kids addicted to warnings.

We have to teach our children we mean what we say the first time.

That was driven home to me when Sam refused to clean up his toys and put away his Lighting McQueen toy.

We told him to pick up all the toys he wanted to keep, as the rest were going to Goodwill. And he called our bluff.

It was sad to see one of his favorite toys dropped off at the consignment store, but I recovered when I discovered how well that worked. Clean-up time is going smoothly at the Hardy house these days.

That's not to say I've mastered all the child-rearing Jedi mind-tricks, thus enjoy a peaceful, tantrum-free existence. Ironically, the night we got our certificates for completing the course, Sam had an epic meltdown on the walk home.

He ended up taking me and his brother, who was in my arms, to the ground. And I demonstrated the extreme opposite of calm, empathetic parenting as we tumbled in our concrete driveway.

After a tearful, drawn-out bedtime for all of us, I found comfort in my favorite quote by Mary Anne Radmacher, "Courage doesn't always roar. Sometimes courage is the quiet voice at the end of the day saying, 'I will try again tomorrow.'"

The next morning, I apologized to Sam for getting so angry with him and he apologized for "being nasty." I decided to keep my crumpled certificate as a reminder that I get to try my parenting practice again tomorrow—or in 10 minutes, whichever the case may be.

Lessons learned on the park circuit

JUL 6

After a few years on the local park circuit, I have the answer to the oft-asked question: "Can't we all just get along?"

Nope.

But that's actually good news, because playgrounds are a prime breeding ground for both germs and personal growth opportunities.

At Discovery Park, I watched a pre-teen girl take something right out of my son's hand. When I called her on it, she lied.

Mature mom that I am, I took a nasty tone.

"Yes, you did!" I said. "You're lying to my face."

At that point, I realized I could stand down, as the object in question was a plastic cup and I'm not personally responsible for that girl's upbringing—or her karma, for that matter.

I share the story with humility, because I recognize it was a completely inappropriate way to treat a child, no matter the situation. As Maya Angelou said, "When you know better, you do better."

Perhaps some playground rules for parents I've picked up will help save you the embarrassment of overreacting as I did to protect your child from something they've likely already gotten over.

Scenario No. 1: Someone takes something your child was playing with.

Your first response might be: To snatch it right back and say, "So, how does it feel?"

Instead, try: Encouraging your kid to use her words and speak up for herself. Try saying: "Wow, it looks like you're upset he took your toy. Why don't you tell him you didn't like that and ask for it back?"

Because: Sticking up for yourself is a life skill and you're still gently reminding the other child he or she needs to give it back—you are just doing it without being confrontational.

Bonus: You don't end up looking like a jerk.

Scenario No. 2: Kids are walking up the slide instead of sliding down. Your kid wants to do it, too, but you're a stickler about slide rules.

Your first response might be: To tattle to their parents or give them a lecture on slide safety.

Instead, try: Speaking directly to your child, reminding him "We go up the stairs and down the slide."

Because: You're not the world's hall monitor. I'd make an exception, though, for older unsupervised kids, in which case I'd approach them kindly and explain that your kid looks up to big kids and he's not allowed to climb the slide. Ask if they'd mind giving the climbing a break for a bit. This works because you aren't telling them what to do, you're asking for their cooperation in a respectful way.

Bonus: You're still reminding the other kids of the rules, and possibly drawing the other parents' attention in a nice way. This only works, of course, if you avoid a snotty, pointed tone.

Scenario No. 3: Someone else tries to parent your children.

Around kids, things go from good to bad in a blink, so it's easy to miss the reason everyone is suddenly crying. If there are several parents at the playground, you can work together to keep everyone safe and sane, but only if you allow someone else to correct your children as needed.

If you happen to be the kind of parent who is offended by this sort of thing, be sure to look up from your phone often enough to deal with them yourself.

For the record, if you ever see Sam or Jake Hardy ride a bike by your house without a helmet, you have my permission to call them out and send them packing for home. Tell them their mother said so.

Remember, your little darling could be on either side of any of these scenarios, sometimes on the same day. I've seen my boys model perfect sharing, using their words instead of fists and being thoughtful. I've seen my kids get sand thrown in their faces, pushed, bossed around and left out.

I've also seen them grab toys, hog the bottom of the slide, cut in line and make other poor choices. Our reaction to those poor choices is the difference between having a problem or having an opportunity to teach them important social skills by allowing them to "do better" as they grow into themselves.

They said there would be bon-bons

AUG 3

I know telling you a story about what I heard on daytime television perpetuates the cliche of stay-at-home moms eating bon-bons and watching soap operas. For the record, I happened to be on the gym treadmill.

The co-hosts of "The View" were discussing a co-parenting survey released last month by TheBump.com and ForbesWoman.com. I tuned in just in time to hear that moms are equally stressed about their responsibilities, whether they work outside the home or not.

I wish it went without saying that while the stresses might be different, stress is still stress.

Joy Behar, one of the co-hosts, didn't agree. She couldn't fathom what a stay-at-home mother could possibly be stressed about.

"What's the stress? They're bored?"

I couldn't believe I heard that correctly. Did this co-host of a daytime talk show really just do the verbal equivalent of flipping the bird to her target demographic?

So I went online to check. And it got worse.

To stir the proverbial pot, the genius running the show's comment board posted this original, thought-provoking question: "Who has it harder, stay-at-home or working moms?"

Seriously? We're still having this conversation?

I think stay-at-home moms and working mothers are equally necessary.

The debate over which is better is ridiculous at best and sexist, demeaning and damaging at worst. Besides, it's utterly pointless.

People can discuss theories all day, but without understanding all the factors each family must consider, who can really say what is best for someone else?

Being mothers is what we have in common. The measure of a good mother isn't the number of minutes spent with her children; it's the quality of the moments shared that matter.

I started writing a column detailing what it is I do, exactly, that keeps the luxury of boredom at bay. But I couldn't hold it to 600 words.

The condensed version is this: In the business of keeping kids alive and relatively happy all day, the "to-do" list is endless. So that whole bon-bon thing? Yeah, it's crap!

To answer Ms. Behar's question, the stresses of being a stay-at-home mom have nothing to do with being bored and everything to do with the assumptions, expectations and ridiculous assertions like the one she made.

As with any other job, there are positives and negatives. I chose to be home with my children and I love that I am.

My biggest stress—next to the responsibility of keeping two toddlers intent on hurting themselves out of harm's way—is simply this:

The illusion that so many people have about me is that I have complete control of my time, when in actuality it feels like I'm tethered to meeting the needs of two toddlers 24-7. And the fact is that if I complain about the harder parts of my day, I'm not met with the same empathy as others lamenting specific aspects of their jobs.

I don't have room here to get into the maddening shift being a stay-at-home mom can create in the dynamics of a marriage, but according to the survey by TheBump.com and ForbesWoman.com, whether at home with the kids all day or not, "Moms overall say they feel resentful toward their partner because of the unbalanced load of household and parenting responsibilities."

So the next time someone like, say, your husband surveys the debris and wonders what you did all day, hand them this column.

If I could offer one more piece of advice, I think it helps to get to a place where you are OK with being misunderstood, whether it's by a big-mouthed celebrity or your own husband. That being said, if you're frazzled and frustrated, you're not alone; evidently two-thirds of us feel that way.

I suppose I should thank the Joy Behars of America for the compliment. Stay-at-home moms must make it look so easy people think we can afford to be bored.

To see a minute-by-minute look at a day in my life as a stay-at-home mom, visit my blog at www.nathaliesnotes.typepad.com. You'll see that "bored" is the last adjective I'd use to describe myself.

Overwhelmed? Yes. Grateful? Totally. Frustrated? For sure. Blessed? You bet. But bored? Not so much.*

---

*   It dawned on me after the column ran that perhaps Behar meant "bored" as a result

A 'new' mother no more

September 7

I recently found myself Googling "when is a baby no longer a baby," as if I didn't already know.

It was when, instead of leaning into a snuggle, mine said, clear as day, "Dooooooooown!" Or when his sweet, wet "kiss, kiss" was replaced by an equally affectionate head butt.

The head-butting is only one of many signs that my baby has officially become a kid. And that, of course, means I am no longer a "new" mom.

While it's true the shock of each fall, the fear of each fever and the nagging feelings of uncertainty have worn off, the awe and awkwardness at each new phase of my boys' development hasn't faded at all. In fact, my amazement at the opportunity to be their mother continues to grow alongside them.

We say "new" mom, but is there even such a thing as a "seasoned" one? Even with five kids, wouldn't there be things to learn, adjustments to make, personalities to factor in and so on?

I imagine the mom whose baby is just starting kindergarten, or the mother whose daughter is just learning to drive, or the mother whose son is starting college are all feeling pretty "new" as they experience yet another phase on the path of parenting.

Parenting isn't an Xbox 360 game. There is no such thing as "expert-level" parents.

So how, besides the aforementioned head-butting, did I know I was growing out of my "new mom" status? When I heard the unmistakable sound of a newborn baby crying, and I felt a pang of longing instead of a flashback of panic.

I know now that when people said "enjoy every moment," they didn't mean I should be grateful to be covered in rank-smelling spit up, but rather that one day I would smile at the memory. They simply knew that those rapidly moving early days would fade into memories as fast as my boys outgrew their sweet baby clothes.

The actual moment I graduated from the "new mom" club was when

---

of doing mind-numbing tasks and routine chores all day long, rather than "bored" meaning you have nothing to do. But I either way, it's not the right adjective in my experience.

I saw a onesie that said, "My mommy doesn't want your advice."

I immediately thought, "Where was that when I had babies?" That led to: "I no longer have babies!" Then to: "And now I have all this advice to share!"

I know, I know. Long-time readers of this column will appreciate the irony of me writing in defense of unsolicited advice.

It's just that I didn't understand what possessed complete strangers to offer it to me in such intimate places as the bulk foods section at WinCo until I found myself stalking this pregnant woman with a bewildered look on her face in Target's baby-gear aisles.

I admit, I thought people who offered all that advice were being know-it-alls. That is, until I found myself wanting to tell this woman she didn't need even half that stuff she was buying.

I wanted to tell her that her favorite moments with baby would include none of the things on the list she was consulting. I wanted to tell her that what mattered more than who comes to the baby shower is who shows up for you after the baby actually arrives.

I wanted to tell her that this experience would, indeed, turn her world upside down, but she would love the view from there. I wanted to tell her this would be harder than she thought, but she was stronger than she could imagine.

I said none of this. I did smile and hover nearby for a moment, in case she had any questions. But she either didn't have any or she was saving them for someone wearing a red employee T-shirt.

I went on minding my own business, marveling at the idea that I'd become one of those annoying advice-givers, even only in my own mind.

I should've told her to get the onesie. Even though it wouldn't halt the avalanche of advice, it would bring some humor to the conversation.

So, to those of you at the starting line of motherhood—especially to my dear friend Stephanie—congratulations! And while I promise to hold back the unsolicited kind of advice, you know how to reach me.

Getting back to birthday basics

OCT 8

I did not enjoy my son's third birthday party. Of course, I was happy to mark the milestone, but the celebration itself was pure madness.

Because I'd avoided the traditional birthday mayhem for Sam's first two years of life, I figured it was time to add hosting birthday parties to my mommy-do list.

A simple Google search for party ideas revealed that old-school parties featuring cupcakes and games like hot potato and duck-duck-goose have been replaced by elaborate theme-based extravaganzas with cakes sculpted into images of the guest of honor and expensive entertainment in the form of rented carnivals, merry-go-rounds and petting zoos.

Because it seemed like the thing to do, I went ahead and planned a modern-day birthday party at a pumpkin patch. In October. On a Saturday.

What was I thinking? Sam and I have a low threshold for crowds and chaos, and his party included too much of both.

As my mother-in-law and I schlepped the gifts, leftover sheet cake and Crock-Pot back to the car, she casually mentioned that her kids had parties at home, with just a few friends. Genius!

It was an expensive but valuable lesson for me. Instead of worrying about throwing my kids The Best Birthday Party Ever, my focus should have been on teaching them the gift of enjoying life within our means.

Since children learn most from the attitude with which we approach things, I'm cheerfully going back to birthday basics this year. I'm keeping things simple and inviting only as many kids as there are candles.

My modern twist might include e-mailed invitations and a homemade pin-the-hood on "Mater" game.

I thought I had found the perfect theme to match Sam's interests and my budget in camping. And it was, until I hit Google for some inspiration.

If parenting is a competitive sport, the camping-theme birthday party I found called "Camp Luke" takes the cake for "most over-the-top" (at least in the noncelebrity division), "most expensive favors" (L.L. Bean backpacks for each child, loaded with camping gear) and "most likely to make the other parents feel like crap" (no explanation necessary). But that's only if you buy into the whole competition thing.

Luckily for those of us who don't have the means to create our own elaborate Camp Luke, going "retro" is in. So it's actually cool to entertain kids with the (free) games we used to play.

Sardines or kick the can anyone? I might even get really crazy and let the kids use their own imaginations.

I saw an example of this recently where my friend Sofia, the birthday girl, raided the towel bin and set up a star-gazing activity for her friends. It was perfect.

I might not be the mom who makes the best birthday cake on the block, or hand-crafts invitations. But you know what? I am the kind of mom who searches yard sales, consignment stores and Craigslist for the perfect train-table crane.

I'm also the kind of mom who makes sure Sam has rain boots that fit in time for his big day, so we can go on the Ultimate Puddle Stomp together. I'm also the kind of mom who uses cookie cutters on pancakes and food coloring in the bathtub, because I know fun things can make a kid feel pretty special.

Isn't that the whole point anyway?

If my kids ever happen to wonder why we never took out a loan for their birthday celebrations, I will know something went wrong in their upbringing. I will tell them:

I gave you the gift of life. What you do with it is your gift back to the world. All the rest is just icing on the cake.

A little gratitude goes a long way

NOV 2

As I ride the merry-go-round of motherhood, I find fodder for this column everywhere—from news items I'm compelled to address, from Kelly Ripa getting under my skin or from my darling kids doing something that forces me to call poison control. Twice. In the same week.

I also dial into God for inspiration, and perhaps for a little help meeting my deadline, in the form of smooth days with soundly sleeping children.

This month, I planned to write about teaching kids gratitude.

But I started worrying that God hadn't gotten around to checking voicemail, because it just wasn't coming together. The more I wrote, the more I realized that actual gratitude is more than just good manners.

It can't be taught. It must be practiced, even when it's not convenient.

To be grateful when your child calls you out of a deep sleep at 3 a.m. for the third night in a row seems like a lot to ask. But that's what happened when I sent God a more urgent message, reminding him of my deadline.

Would I have preferred to be writing about the amazing windfall that arrived the very next day, rendering me eternally grateful?

Sure. But this is real life.

When Jake's middle-of-the-night monkey business woke me up, I was ticked. That is, I was until I started rocking him and he cuddled up, wrapped one of his little hands around my neck and shoved his stinky Zebra in my face with the other.

I realized I had my answer. I have to be grateful instead of grumpy, even when it's not the obvious response. A feeling of love and gratitude filled me as I rocked my baby and let my thoughts wander to two local boys I will never meet—Cody Myers and Jacob Rowan.

I am sure their mothers would do just about anything to be awakened in the middle of the night by their babies. Jacob's mom said she was grateful for every minute she got with her baby, all 33 of them.

Of course, I don't think it's fair or reasonable to ask someone to contemplate their blessings in the midst of despair. But when we turn our focus to the positive side of things, healing happens.

This is not to say we pretend our problems don't exist or bury our grief, rather that we cultivate a conscious thankfulness anyway.

Naturally, the more we do it ourselves, the more likely our children are to count their blessings instead of their complaints. Here are a few, simple exercises I teach in my journaling class to help people get out of the culture of complaining and begin realizing how blessed they actually are:

1. A cheap notebook can yield a gold mine of perspective if you make it a regular practice to end your days by jotting down a few things you're grateful for.

2. Make it a habit to say some kind of blessing at mealtimes. Even better, ask members of your family to participate by sharing one thing they're thankful for that day.

3. Let your kids see your gratitude in action. Express appreciation for a good parking spot instead of complaining about the crowded lot.

4. Go out of your way to be grateful. Tell a manager about a positive interaction with an employee. Write a thank you note to someone who went out of their way for you and mail it to them. Yes, in the mail.

5. Even after a trying day, or perhaps especially after a trying day, tell your child something you appreciate about him or her. Why not make a point to do this every day at bed time?

These simple actions are powerful beyond measure. They stir the heart and shift our consciousness.

As Meister Eckhart famously said, "If the only prayer you said in your whole life was, 'Thank you,' that would suffice."

Family values not something you can buy

DEC 7

Two things you wouldn't think go well together have merged into the makings of a very merry Christmas season at the Hardy household.

With some job changes, and my husband building a new business from scratch, we don't exactly have a "Christmas budget."

Combine financial reality with the fact that my 4-year-old is at that magical stage where this time of year is full of awe and wonder and you've got a recipe for several potentially stressful weeks.

As Sam's mom, I'm in charge of making sure Santa delivers, all while simultaneously teaching him what we believe this time of year is really all about Baby Jesus.

It turns out that with Jesus in my heart and Santa in my imagination, I already have everything I need to make that magic happen. The truth is, I haven't been this excited about Christmas since I was a kid.

I know I'm not the only one making merry on a minimal budget, so I'll share my holiday hacks and hope you'll do the same in return.

It's important to keep in mind that being festive doesn't need to be fancy. If you think about the traditions you value from your own childhood, I'd be willing to wager they weren't pricey, but produced priceless memories nonetheless.

A good place to start is by, well, starting. The sooner you begin nailing down holiday details, the less you'll spend.

You can use this newspaper to scout out bargains at local stores and create a festive schedule of free events, allowing you to pop a dinner from the freezer into the oven on busy evenings.

In addition to participating in the season's festivities, try to find small ways to build up to the big celebration all month long. After all, it's the little, fun things you do that add up to make meaningful memories.

You being truly present, instead of frantically out trying to find the perfect present to purchase, is what sets the tone for your family's holidays.

If you have cookie cutters and bread, you have the makings for special touches for toast and sandwiches.

Simple can be delightful to a little kid. You can add a few drops of food coloring to bath water, put sprinkles on popcorn and stir cocoa with candy canes.

To keep things festive, consider inviting Elf on the Shelf into your home. Essentially this elf serves as Santa's little narc, flying to the North Pole at night to report his findings and re-appearing in the morning in a new spot, perhaps having wreaked a little havoc along the way.

This morning, our elf decorated framed photos with a Dry Erase marker. Sam observed, "Finn can do things we aren't allowed to do."

If I'd known participating in the whole Elf on the Shelf business would mean more work for me, I might not have been so eager to invite that mischievous little sprite into our life. But ever since our elf, Finn, arrived at Thanksgiving, I've enjoyed planning ways to delight my kids when they go looking for him the first thing every morning.

I love being able to partner up with my husband in creating an atmosphere of playfulness. It makes this side of Santa's world fun.

Just scouring ads for sales on more things we don't truly need isn't very fulfilling. Joy, on the other hand, is something we can all use more of.

I'm still at the beginning of continuing traditions from my childhood and creating new ones. I would enjoy hearing what you've done, or are doing, to create lasting memories of your own with your family.

Merry Christmas from mine to yours!

Meditating through the mayhem

JAN 4

Anyone who's spent much time with small children knows things can go from calm to chaotic in the time it takes to turn your head. For example, at our house recently, what looked like two happy boys reading abruptly turned into one boy happily reading while the older one played barber and butchered both heads of hair.

As I navigate these moments between peace and pandemonium, I want to be more Zen, less banshee. So I try to do things like yoga to keep my sanity from simmering over, but with two little guys, our yoga sessions morph quickly into less calming judo matches.

Then there's meditation. Learning to meditate has been a revolving resolution of mine. I know some people think it's easy, but I can't think of many things more challenging than sitting still and doing nothing— not even thinking—for two minutes, much less the typically recommended 20.

While trying to talk to a friend about ways to incorporate meditation into our days, we were interrupted three times. During the first Pilates class I tried, I was called back to the child-care center 45 seconds into a two-minute plank.

Admittedly, I was kind of thankful for that one, but still it's frustrating not to be able to figure out something that I know would be beneficial to my health. After touting the myriad benefits of meditation, magazine articles often suggest people "just carve out at least 20 minutes a day." But from where, exactly?

My kids are little. I love them being little. I don't want to wish them out of diapers and needing me this much, because I know if I'm not careful I'll have wished away their whole childhood. It's already passing by too quickly.

What I have to find is a way to incorporate aspects of a meditation practice into my life as it is right now. I've learned that inner peace is possible only when you give in to fully embracing your life exactly as it is instead of lamenting the one you thought you would, or should, have.

I had an epiphany just before Christmas. I had a long list of things I needed to do after the boys went to bed. Except they wouldn't go to sleep. Jake was crying for me to snuggle him and Sam said he was afraid to be alone. It had already been a long day and I couldn't handle a battle of wills. So I took a deep breath, piled my tearful kids into bed and snuggled them until their sobs subsided.

I waited until I felt the fingers clinging to my neck release their grip. As I breathed through those minutes, I realized in the course of going about my business mothering, I'd found a way to meditate in the moment instead of wishing it away. Being present in the moment, listening to their breathing, feeling their bodies relax beside me changed me.

When I untangled myself, I didn't find the dishes magically done or the gifts wrapped and packed into the car. I did, however, approach each of those tasks differently. I'd experienced my own shift from trying to manage everything, and everyone, to get to the next thing on my list to just riding the wave I was on until it was time to catch the next one.

Four years into my mommy gig, I think I've figured out the trick to keeping my head out of the proverbial oven: Instead of resisting them, ride the waves as they come. For now, my yoga studio will have to be in my head and my heart. At last, this meditating mama is breathing through the mayhem, one wave at a time.

When self-esteem erodes, fix is within

FEB 1

During this season of commercially artificial love, I want to address a kind of love that eludes many of us but is the only solid foundation for genuine love: self-love. Saccharin as it may sound, loving ourselves is the key to loving our partners, our children, our family and friends in the fullest sense of the word.

I've often heard it said that the best thing a father can do for his children is love their mother. I think it's also true that the best thing a mother can do for her family is love herself.

Motherhood, even with all of its blessings, can erode self-esteem—especially if it was fragile to begin with.

It seems from the e-mails I've received that there is an epidemic of low self-esteem among women, many of them mothers. We have to change this attitude, both for ourselves and for the children we are raising to become confident, competent adults.

Life is precious. It's short. And it can be hard and cruel, even if we don't add to our own suffering.

It's also amazing and delightful, of course. But that's easy for us to miss if we're busy counting our faults instead of celebrating ourselves exactly the way we are.

Contrary to the media messages we receive, we deserve to like ourselves without achieving, fixing, surgically removing, surgically adding, cosmetically repairing or radically changing anything.

We think we need all this self-improvement to be more at ease with ourselves, but I believe a deep sense of self-worth is the only workable foundation, so that's where to put the focus.

Once you are OK with you the way you are, you can go about tweaking whatever you want more of or less of in your life. Otherwise, you're just making cosmetic improvements.

Of course, you can't pick up a pack of self-esteem at Target. Maybe you had it once and you lost touch with it. Maybe you think it might be too late. Or perhaps you say, "I've always been like this. I can't change."

At a young age, I learned to compare myself to others and catalog where I didn't measure up. I learned to use that as evidence of my unworthiness.

That type of chronic thinking landed me on a therapist's couch. Luckily, I realized there had to be a better way to live this one, short, precious life than by going around counting the ways I sucked.

I share this not because it's comfortable, but because I know I'm not alone. During my self-help odyssey to recalibrate my "normal," I realized that more than anything, so many of us are seeking validation that we are normal. Even the darkest parts of our souls need the light of recognition.

It turns out you get confidence by earning it from, get a load of this, yourself! Once you have your own approval, no one else's will be enough.

I promise this is true. Deep down, I think we all know it is.

That's where keeping a journal comes in handy. It is a rare person who has an unobstructed view of himself or herself.

Your worth is not measured by your mother, your mother-in-law, your job, your lack of a job, your husband, your lack of a husband, your skinny jeans or your fat pants. Your worth is measured by you.

A written record of your accomplishments, fears and struggles helps you be more accurate than relying solely on memories of your failures and the worst things people have said and done to you.

One step toward increasing your own self-worth is to do the things you love. Pick something you can do in pockets of time. Try something new, even if, or especially if, you don't think you'll do it as well as anyone else.

Let yourself be a beginner. Think of it as your opportunity to impress your own self. And as practice for giving the finger to the part of you that says you can't. For example, even though I'd be much better at Zumba with a few cocktails in me, I've been trying it at the gym and am actually enjoying exercising.

Finally, find your "reset" button. When I start feeling all kinds of angsty, one of two things always helps: journaling or physically moving through it with a workout, a quick walk or dancing with my kids to something other than Muppet music.

As George Eliot famously said, it is never too late to be what you might have been. This year for Valentine's Day give yourself the sweetest gift of investing in yourself. You're worth it.

Public tries to substitute opinion for information

MAR 7

When Tommy Jordan's daughter dissed him on Facebook, he promised her if it ever happened again, he'd shoot a bullet through her laptop. Good thing he didn't threaten to take away her birthday, because a few weeks ago it did, indeed, happen again.

I have kind of a bleeding heart, so many of my friends assumed I'd be appalled by this North Carolina dad's shock and awe campaign, aimed at his teenager. Actually, though, I couldn't help but applaud when I saw this accidentally-gone-viral video.

After spending many hours and $130 upgrading his 15-year-old daughter's computer, Tommy Jordan found an obnoxious, disrespectful letter she'd posted for her friends on Facebook. She tried to hide it from her parents, but unfortunately for her, her dad makes a living in the IT industry.

He found a way to communicate to her, and her friends, that there was nothing cute, funny or acceptable about her attitude.

He created an eight minute YouTube video in which he read her letter, while interjecting his own reactions (particularly objecting to her insistence on being paid to do chores) and corrections (he does not, in fact, expect her to pick up after her parents, just herself). Then he fired a bullet into her laptop—the one he'd just spent a lot of his own time and money upgrading—and posted the video to her Facebook page.

Message sent—except for one small problem.

While the video was intended only for a small audience, it has now been viewed by more than 30 million people. And some had strong reactions, ranging from reporting him to Child Protective Services to urging him to run for president.

There's no doubt Tommy Jordan hit a nerve. If the responders weren't attacking him, they were making awful assumptions about a young girl they knew nothing about aside from this one, embarrassing thing.

Even if you watched the entire video, eight minutes does not tell the full story. Whether criticizing the dad's actions or commending him by condemning her, the whole conversation is misguided.

The dude didn't mean to hang his daughter out to dry. He loves her, or else he wouldn't care. He loves her, or else he wouldn't be trying to do something about her attitude of entitlement.

I'm not defending what Tommy Jordan did as much as I am his right to do it. My impression, from following the journey of his Facebook fiasco, is that this is a close family that is managing to weather the ensuing storm of public opinion together.

What I am concerned about is the ironic lesson learned in all of this: What you put online stays online. Forever. There's no pulling back.

Instead of debating differing opinions on taking a .45 to his kid's laptop, we should be focusing on what this guy has to say about keeping our children safe online. Because while Tommy Jordan never claimed to be a parenting expert, this shoot-from-the-hip dad is knowledgeable—and eloquent—on issues relating to Internet safety for children.

Parenting is personal.

Would I do the same thing Tommy Jordan did? Probably not. It's more my style to revoke my kid's right to use the electricity I pay for.

But to each his own, as long as no harm is done. And "harm" isn't something that can be gauged in the court of public opinion.

It seems lately that we regard an opinion as a good substitute for information. It isn't.

I'd love to hear people say in response to insipid, contrived questions like, "Is what Tommy Jordan did appropriate or abusive?" with an honest, "I'm not sure, because I don't know the whole story." You can't look at a snapshot of someone's parenting taken at a desperate moment and determine what kind of parent—or person—he is.

What you can do, though, is consider what kind of parent you want to be. What you can do is learn from your mistakes, as well as the mistakes of others. That and never underestimate the power of the Internet.

How will you fight bullying?

APR 4

A movie called "Bully" was released last week without a rating. After the Motion Picture Association of America gave it an R rating due to some foul language, the Weinstein Co. decided to leave it up to individual theaters to decide how to handle its showing.

Here's the thing: Swearing might be uncomfortable, but it is a reality that the 13 million children who are bullied every year have to live with. So parents get to be parents and decide if they are going to let their children see this movie.

Personally, I would rather have my kids watch a movie like "Bully," cursing and all, than some of the television fare targeting young kids. Because this movie is real.

I am not afraid for my boys to know life can be hard. They have to know that in order to know they can deal with it.

Bullying is a serious, insidious problem in classrooms and online. It can happen, it does happen and it's happening right now.

According to the Bully Project, in the seven minutes since you picked up this paper, a child has been bullied on a playground somewhere in America. Was it yours?

Watching a movie like this as a family can pave the way for conversations that might not happen otherwise. The associated website, located at http://thebullyproject.com, has more resources to guide parents and teachers in taking this opportunity for a meaningful discussion.

Since we can't know everything that is said to our kids when they're away from us, it's important to make sure we are offsetting any negative messages they receive with the truth about themselves.

I don't mean the false, empty kind. I am talking about genuine, personalized praise.

Whether you do it at breakfast, bedtime or by text, make sure you are regularly telling your kids something positive about them every single day.

Before I tell Sam my thing for the day, I ask if there's anything he's particularly proud of. Often he shares something he's not proud of at all and we get a chance to talk about how everyone makes mistakes and we look for the lesson in it.

I think that is a life skill as important as tying shoes. More so, because there is no Velcro on the market to fix poor self-esteem.

So maybe your kid isn't being bullied, nor is he bullying others. While that is wonderful, you aren't absolved of your responsibility to make sure they understand what it is and how to handle it when they see it happening. By our silence, we condone what's happening.

Teach your kids how to stand up for themselves and for others. Remind them that even the meanest of kids actually needs help. Staying silent protects no one.

As dangerous as not speaking up is the "kids will be kids" posture, based on the assumption no harm really comes of all this bullying business. It's common to hear people dismiss bullying by arguing that it's been going on forever and—this is my favorite part—we turned out OK.

Well, no, we didn't.

Being bullied shapes a person. It leaves a lasting impact. I know, because as a child, I was spit on, called names, physically beaten, intimidated, harassed and humiliated until I wanted to kill myself.

Much later, I still avoided eating in the school cafeteria for nearly a year before the school secretary finally talked me into making that walk across campus.

You should know that by then, I was well into my adulthood and the school secretary, Mrs. Hess, was a co-worker.

That's right. Even at the age of 30, I would rather go hungry than return to the torture chamber of my childhood.

While the scars from bullying last forever, the opportunity to stop bullying presents itself daily. Take it.

Stand up for yourself, your children and for the ones who can't. Do it so yours don't suffer and the ones who did didn't do it in vain.

Still rewriting the story of me

MAY 5

Whether you grow up in Disneyland or Dysfunction Junction, friction is a natural part of family life. Who doesn't have moments when they look around the dinner table and wonder how they could possibly be related to these people?

Imagine my surprise when I found out, 21 years ago, that this occasional passing fantasy was actually fact in my case.

Let me set the stage for you. It was my freshman year in high school. The assignment was to write an autobiography, with the incentive of extra credit for creativity.

I decided to use a picture of my mom, pregnant with me, for the cover. But I couldn't find any such picture.

I tried to substitute one from the period my mom was pregnant with my brother. None of those existed either.

I found it difficult to believe my father, who even takes pictures of his food[*], didn't have a working camera available during a pair of nine-month spans.[**] So, overachiever that I was, I had no choice but to take my project to the next level.

When my parents were out one evening, I went into reporter mode, snooping through my mom's red address book. One by one, I called close family friends to announce I was doing a project for school.

Naturally, they were all happy to help. That is, until I asked: "Could you tell me your favorite memory of my mom pregnant?"

Whether by hesitation, an awkward pause or the sharp inhalation of surprise, my suspicions were confirmed.

A couple of them wanted to know if my mom knew about this project. She sure didn't, but this was pre-cell phone, so no one could text my parents a heads up.

---

[*]   It's worth noting my dad's been taking picture of food since way before social media made that a thing. He used to pay to develop an entire roll of film[**] to get one good shot of a goulash kettle.

[**] In the olden days film is something people used to have processed and wait for before seeing how their pictures turned out. There used to be a thing called "wasting film." Hence, food photos weren't really a fad. Fun Fact: There used to be such a thing as drive-through film processing. For real. That was before you could get a 16 ounce, white-chocolate peppermint mocha with soy milk every twelve blocks though.

Why didn't I simply ask my parents? I did in 1991, and purely by coincidence, it was on Mother's Day.

After a painfully awkward brunch on Bainbridge Island, and a silent drive home, my parents finally told me the truth about my birth.

I felt as if my foundation had cracked.

In retrospect I wonder what that news changed exactly. I mean, besides where I spent my first week of life, everything else was the same.

But it wasn't. Not really.

I wish I could tell you I handled the situation with grace and understanding. But, alas, I was 14. So there was plenty of drama.

Unconsciously, I started to ignore the idea that my parents loved me and instead dwell on the fact that someone I'd never met didn't—at least not enough to keep me.

Now I understand the best way my birth mother could show her love was by acknowledging she couldn't do for me what my parents could. But back then, I started telling myself the secret truth about me was that I was simply unlovable.

This became a core belief of mine, one I sought out and affirmed in my relationships.

It wasn't until very recently that I learned the story I was telling myself wasn't true. How could I have been so wrong about something I was so certain about?

The thing about our birth stories is that they're just that: stories. The meaning we give the story is what matters.

I could focus on the fact that nobody was with me during the first week of my life, or I could instead remember that my parents canceled a ski trip to come and get me as soon as they heard they could.

At every birthday since, I've heard that story. And it delights me every single time.

I don't know very much about my biological mom, besides the fact that she was an Irish X-ray technician with four children.

But I can tell you my real mom has cutting boards stained green with parsley, can make goulash in her sleep, has fingers calloused from a lifetime of hard work yet still capable of soothing a feverish forehead, keeps her nails clean and cuticles trimmed, has a favorite apron in green, and smells like Gucci and geraniums.

She is probably reading this with tears in her eyes.

She should know that while I'm sorry for that one awful Mother's Day, I have loved her as my real and only mom on every one of them before and since.

By the way, I did get extra credit for my bonus chapter: "My Adoption." I like to think of that as my first investigative reporting piece, inspiring a career in journalism.

Mealtime wrangling worth the effort

JUN 6

Most moms I know dread dinner. There's the planning it, preparing it, negotiating the eating of it and, finally, cleaning up the aftermath.

The fact that kids want dinner every single night exacerbates the problem. Parents are charged with creating nutritive, nourishing mealtimes, complete with engaging family conversations, and doing it again and again.

While I'm sure most of us want to succeed as nutritionists to our offspring, and make lasting mealtime memories, it's hard to do either when dealing with picky eaters and delivering stimulating one-liners such as: "Please don't poke your brother with your fork;" "Please just try one bite; it won't kill you."

That's not to mention the constant reminders to use good manners - or any at all. When all is said and done, you have to wonder if it's worth it.

But, of course, it is.

Research backs up the value of family meals in multiple areas, including health, esteem and sense of belonging. If you can survive them, regular meals together forge stronger family bonds.

So we try.

Sometimes, we're like a Norman Rockwell painting, only messier. Other times, my boys decide to act like the toddlers they are and randomly go on strike.

Most recently, my 2-year-old decided he wasn't going to eat his vegetables anymore. After a few days of this, his dad and I united in what will forever be known as "The Salad Standoff."

We served salad separately, before the rest of dinner, so there was no room for discussion, debate or drama.

Jake immediately pushed his bowl away. "Don't want 'dat," he announced.

We calmly explained he had to eat his salad—like the rest of us. Then he could have dinner, which would be followed by dessert.

The rest of us ate in that order, while Jake refused to take a single bite of salad.

He kept repeating "I don't like salad! 'Dat yucky!" until we finally excused him from the table. By then, we were all done eating.

I was worried about how the night would go, but was confident in our choice to starve him out to teach him a healthy habit. For the record, there was nothing in that salad he hasn't eaten and liked before—spinach, sprouts, goat cheese, sunflower seeds and the dressing he loves.

I can hear it now: "You'd seriously send your kid to bed hungry because he wouldn't eat his salad?" Totally. Because I'm the mom.

And because I refuse to spend the next 16 years begging people to eat the meals I went out of my way to make for them.

Here's what happened:

As I was putting his pajamas on, Jake looked at me with his big, owl brown eyes and said: "Mama, I hungee."

"Do you want your salad?" I replied.

"Yes," he said.

I tried not to look shocked—or smug—as I carried him back to the table, where his salad was still waiting for him. He happily ate it, followed by two servings of meatloaf and none of mashed potatoes.

File under "battle picking."

Let me be clear:

I do not condone withholding food as a punishment. Not for anything. Not ever.

I do, however, completely support parents in making reasonable, healthy choices for their children. If a child chooses not to eat, so be it.

Show me a child who has intentionally starved himself in the history of ever, and I'll eat my words. Until then, trust me. If they know throwing a fit or otherwise negotiating their way out of it won't work, kids will eventually give in and eat what's for dinner.

Got guilt?

JUL 4

I used to believe guilt was every mother's burden.

Then I started doing something that called that into question on a daily basis. I did something that's become more the norm than the exception for mothers in America—working outside the home.

A month ago, I went back to work after five years of being a stay-at-home mom.

Originally, our plan was for me to stay home until both boys were in school. In fact, when I wrote my column last month, I had no idea this was coming. I only knew that the shoestring we were living on was starting to strangle us.

I started looking into daycare options, just in case something turned up. I made some phone calls, said some prayers for a positive change and prepared my boys for the possibility.

Then I got the call that the job I'd wanted for years was available.

I applied to be a reporter at this paper, after 12 years away. And in a whirlwind process, I got my desk back in the newsroom.

While I was thrilled to get the job, I would be lying if I didn't acknowledge the deep sense of loss I feel for my identity as a stay-at-home mom—ironically, an identity it took me years to adjust to.

That being said, I'm good with my choice. It's what's best for my family. We now have a neat little thing called health insurance, among other necessities.

Initially, while looking into daycare I felt like I was putting the boys in a basket and sending them down the river. But even that worked out for Moses, so I realized they were going to be fine as long as I found the right place.

And I did. I consider the providers partners in parenting and am grateful for them.

That being said, after five years of being attached at the hip, it's disconcerting to find a sticky note reminding me to pick up the dry-cleaning—and the boys.

There are some shallower changes as well.

For example, instead of making do with my "pony-tail as pen

holder" hairstyle, I've learned to use a curling iron. That caused our first job-related injury when Sam burned his arm on this new foreign object when it appeared in our only bathroom.

And some new phrases have crept into my vocabulary.

After immersing myself in weeks of county budget talks, I told Sam I would put a dollar into his "squirt gun fund." He looked at me oddly and laughed. "Mama! Don't you mean piggy bank?"

A social life and exercise are two things I'm having a hard time working into this new gig.

I began to set my gym clothes and shoes by the door the night before my first day. Every night, as I set my alarm for 5 a.m., I announce I'm planning to go jogging in the morning. But it hasn't happened yet.

We now use "jogging" as a euphemism for "I have no intention of doing that." As in, "I'll read that while you're jogging."

The most stressful thing so far is staying up at night with boys who seem to be coming down with something and wondering, with two new jobs between us, which of us is going to call in sick. I used to be able to shrug off long nights with sick kids as part of the package, but now I'm sweating at the first sign of snot.

So while this transition isn't easy, it's awesome. I believe the attitude with which we do anything is how we do everything. How can I teach my boys to embrace opportunities and have a healthy sense of adventure if I don't demonstrate what that looks like?

Yes, change can be hard. But it's one of life's few constants. Our attitudes determine our conditions, so I'm careful to keep mine positive.

I don't miss my boys during the day in an active, aching way. My job doesn't really allow for that sort of ruminating. Plus, I truly love being a reporter. It's just that I wish I could have both at the same time.

When Sam says, "I'm happy because I'm at daycare, but I'm not happy I can't see you; I feel that way at the same time," it sums up exactly how I feel about this whole reporter mama thing.

You're welcome, future daughter-in-law. It's looking like my little dudes are going to be capable of holding simultaneous emotions and expressing them.

So about that guilt business?

I'm starting to think it's a choice. And I'm not having any part of it.

Planning key to balancing act

JUL 28

Unfortunately, when I went back to work, we lost our housekeeper, chef and chief errand runner. Since the whole division of labor dispute is more contentious than any other parenting issue, let's just say: No amount of sticky notes can get my husband to do things the way I would do them.

That implies I think my way is the correct one—an argument we can have some other day. Regardless of how things get done in any household, certain things have to happen to keep everyone clothed, fed, safe and perhaps even entertained.

I hate to say it, but it comes down to planning. And if planning ahead enables me to still enjoy the view from the hamster wheel that is motherhood, I'll happily break out my Trapper Keeper.

When the person playing the role of, say, stay-at-home mom, adds something like, say, full-time employment to the mix, things have to change to make it all work.

As we work to figure out the new balance of responsibilities around here, I've discovered a few tricks. For starters, always wake up before the little darlings, and know what's for dinner before you start on breakfast.

I know it sounds like I'm channeling June Cleaver, but I promise that me and my floors are too crunchy to pull that off. I just know that doing those two things consistently significantly reduces morning mayhem and subsequent mealtime meltdowns.

Because it's stressful to recreate the meal every night, I don't. I've finally embraced meal planning because I realized it didn't have to mean making dumplings from scratch. My meal planning goes like this: Every Monday we have "haystacks," and the same ingredients get worked into tacos on Wednesday. Tuesday features some kind of stir fry, Thursday some kind of pasta dish.

Friday's themed meal is: figure it out with whatever's left in the fridge.

Over the weekend, I cook batches of rice, beans and chicken, and chop some vegetables. Whoever gets home first can assemble, heat and serve.

Speaking of my refrigerator, it's now covered in artwork. Since starting daycare, my boys have become even more prolific artists then they were before. And now that I'm not with them all day, I feel guiltier throwing it out.

Sam seems to always bust me when I relegate his his art in the recycle bin anyway. The first few times, he assumed it was an accident, but now he watches carefully as I transport his art from the car to the counter, in case I make any false move.

In addition to enjoying my pretend Pottery Barn life on Pinterest, I also get awesome ideas like this one: Take a picture of his art work and create a photo book for him. A few favorites I'll keep in our "Project Life" album and the rest I'll sneak out to the recycle bin after bedtime, burying it under newspapers.

I took the concept a step farther, causing my husband to make The Face, when I asked him if he cared if we had Sam's birthday party on a Saturday or Sunday. In October.

I explained that giving the kids fun parties is important to me, and the only way to do it on a reasonable budget is to plan ahead—way ahead. So I am.

After all, I'll need proof that I was a good mom, to counter what they tell the therapists.

While I'm at it, I've been picking up Christmas-themed books at garage sales this summer. I'm hoping to find 25 to wrap and put out December 1. That way, we can unwrap and read one every evening until we celebrate Christmas.

Yeah, I saw that on Pinterest too. That's not the kind of thing you can pull off cheaply at the last minute, and the memories will be worth it.

Well, that's the fun stuff. But since parents are charged with keeping kiddos safe as well, we need to think about what happens when we get a "boil water" notice because E. coli has been discovered in our water supply. It happened to 135,000 households west of the Willamette a couple weeks ago. Would you have been prepared?

It's easy to stock up a little at a time to build an emergency kit. The art of planning ahead transforms an emergency into a mere inconvenience.

As I strive toward the elusive work-life-balance thing people talk about, I might still be running on the hamster wheel but, all this planning certainly makes me a much happier little hamster mama.

Consequences negative ... and positive

I've heard it said there are two kinds of kids: teenagers and those who will become teenagers.

Since my kids are still under the age of five, it's tempting to laugh that off. It's tempting to ignore the ramifications of today's interactions on their future behavior.

Alas, as parents, we don't have the luxury of pretending time won't turn our little ones into young adults in the blink of an eye.

So, there's a lot to consider in-between the toddler and teenage years. I started to contemplate all this when, during the course of my job, I found myself interviewing a woman whose home was destroyed by a young drunk driver, and later the same week, interviewing the staff of the county's juvenile detention program.

It was not lost on me that my son had just gotten his first "red card" for misbehavior at daycare.

The fact that he got into trouble wasn't so much of an issue for me. He's a kid. He's still learning the rules.

However, Sam's cavalier attitude about it was cause for concern. My little boy not only had the nerve to tell me, "It wasn't a big deal," but also to add, "Besides, red is my favorite color anyway."

In retrospect, his ability to spin the story so readily suggests a successful future in politics.

At the time, Sam surprised me on the way home by saying: "It's really OK, Mama. You said it's good to make mistakes because you learn from them. Didn't you say that? Mama?"

I was quiet, trying to find the right words, but he'd found them for me.

"Yes, that's exactly right, Sammy," I started slowly, watching him through the rearview mirror. "But here's the thing, I'm OK with you making mistakes as long as you learn from them.

"The fact that you still had a red card at the end of the day tells me that not only did you not learn from your mistake, you didn't bother to correct it. I know for a fact that your teachers gave you ample opportunity to earn back a green card."

No answer came from the backseat as he looked out the window the rest of the way home.

Finally, he asked what was going to happen next. I told him his dad and I would figure out something that would help him remember he had to work on making good choices as often as possible.

Matt came up with the idea of a consequence bike.

We had picked it up for free and were planning to give it to Sam. But we decided to make him earn it by proving he was capable of earning green cards regularly.

Sam earned that bike in no time, and we put the red card incidents behind us. Yes, plural, because it took him more than once, it seems, to learn we were serious.

I thought things were going well until day care sent home a baggie full of broken crayons in Sam's lunch box.

I went to him with the baggie and The Face. He responded with a shrug.

I waited. Eventually, he admitted to having broken them—on purpose.

It's important that kids know you love them even when they mess up. That being said, they should know you also love them enough to make sure they make good on their responsibilities.

Sam's been saving up for a squirt gun for the better part of the summer. I could buy it for him, but he doesn't really need it. He just really wants it.

He's been asking for extra chores here and there so he can augment his "squirt gun fund." Sadly, he had to take two hard-earned dollars out of his fund to pay for replacement crayons, though.

It's easy to question whether I'm doing all the right things at all the right times. Easy, and not a bit fun. In fact, it kind of sucks.

But it's nice to know that even if I don't do it all right, my intentions are good.

We are all learning from our mistakes. If we're lucky, we all get little signs along the way that we're on the right track.

While making dinner the day of the crayon pay-off, I heard a clunking sound coming down the stairs. It was Sam, armed with a broom and dustpan, sweeping the stairs.

That was one of those signs.

I recently heard this admonition for parents from one of my favorite writers, Glennon Melton, and I try to keep it in mind: "Don't be so busy trying to raise a good kid that you forget you already have one."

Whirlwind trip worthwhile

When my husband proposed a 500-mile round-trip to his hometown of Walla Walla last weekend, my answer came easily. Nope.

To ease the blow, I suggested we wait until we had a long weekend we could use. But with two new jobs between us, that's a long way out.

I was winning the debate until he said: "Even if it's just for a day, that's one day the boys get to spend with their grandparents." He raised his eyebrows as if to say, "Top that!"

Of course, I couldn't. So that's how I found myself at the bottom of Rex Hill, five minutes into our five-hour drive, answering the "are we there yet" question.

My annoyance softened when I called my mother-in-law to let her know we'd just left town and would be arriving around midnight. She said she knew how Matt gets hungry late at night, so would have a roast waiting for us.

Suddenly, it dawned on me that in what will feel like a blink, I'll be hoping my boys come home with their families. I say it'll feel like a blink, because my baby, Sam, is a week away from turning 5, and is already saying things like: "Mama, when I'm older, I'm going to play football. And I'm going to drive. And I'm going to get a hot rod." After recovering from my panic attack, I wonder why we can't just stick to playing catch and Hot Wheels.

My little guy, Jake, is suddenly all about motorcycles. And he's referring to his beloved stuffed Zebra by the much cooler name "Zebes," though it's not lost on me that the mangy animal is still always in sight, even if the little fingers around its neck have loosened their grip.

I looked at the boys, finally passed out in their car seats just beyond The Dalles, and smiled at Jake clutching Zebes in one hand and his Matchbox car in the other. I remember taking this same drive when he was 8 months old and seeing his much smaller fingers wrapped around Zebra's neck.

It doesn't seem that long ago. Yet the way we traveled then was with a loaded minivan full of all the baby gear I could jam in there: play pen, high chair, stroller, extra food, favorite bedding, bedtime music and, heck, even a little bottle of lavender oil. Those of you with "problem sleepers" will understand the lengths I went to in hopes of catching a few hours of sleep while traveling.

Now, one suitcase holds all we need. How long will it take, I wonder, before "are we there yet" becomes a memory that makes me smile instead of cringe?

Once there, we did simple things like going to my nieces' soccer games, playing with cousins and listening to old family stories. The boys got to ride Nana's horses, cruise in Papa's hot rod and play with "cool cars."

The highlight was getting to spend hours playing in the gravel pile.

I'm afraid we left little piles of rocks throughout the house to be remembered by.

Proving my point that time changes one's perspective, my father-in-law told me those little piles of rocks made him smile. And even after just a day and a half of having the boys there, it suddenly seemed very quiet without them.

The best way to get my boys to have memories with their extended family is to use the means we have available to cultivate those relationships, be it through the post office, the Internet or the highway.

All that aside, I must admit my change of heart was self-serving. I believe in a "pay it forward" kind of world. I'm counting on my kids marrying women willing to make the trip back home, too.

I'm even up for making a midnight roast, provided they don't show up on a motorcycle.

Grief laced with gratitude

NOV 6

I've never really been much of an animal lover.

Until six Octobers ago, when I met my 6-week-old little chocolate bundle of furry love, that is. Now, I'm not sure how people live without them.

But I'll have a chance to figure that out, because life has provided my family two lessons in grief this month.

First, a neighbor's toddler was struck by a car and killed in front of our house. Less than two weeks later, our Lucy Baby met the same fate.

While that little pup grew into a 70-pound tornado sometimes called Lucifer, she was my first baby. When I didn't think I could have children of my own, and then even when I did, she was the one who taught me I could love something more than myself.

I learned that when I stood in the rain so she could go to the bathroom, or lost sleep worrying about her injuries, or freaked out as she nearly got struck by a horse, at which point I decided I would wait to have children until bubble wrap was cool to wear.

Obviously, my boys were born in a time when fluorescent fashion came back instead of the more forward-thinking protective daily wear. And now, I find myself wishing for a way to bubble wrap their little hearts as they process and suffer through the grief of losing a beloved pet.

Crazy as she was, we did love her. And she loved us right back.

She also loved butter right off the counter, bathtubs as long as there was no water in them, sticks of any kind, swims anywhere but the bathtub and car trips riding shotgun.

She hated being alone, coming when called, high-pitched sounds and my cooking. The latter is because in our early days together, I was learning to cook, and that smoke alarm is terribly piercing.

As my family mourns together, we all have our own ways of going about it.

Sam, five, says he hears her barking—in heaven. Jake, nearly 3, keeps wanting to go look for her.

I keep explaining to Jake, once again, what happened. And before long, it all slips past him to the point where he wants to know, "Where my Lucy is?"

I tell them we have lots of pictures and memories. Sam said that doesn't help, and he's right, at least at first.

But as the initial shock and immediate grief recede into more of a numbing sense of loss, they do help. Actually, I think they help a lot.

We talk about Lucy every night at bedtime, and on the way to daycare. Crazy things she did, cute things she did. Sometimes we laugh, sometimes there are tears and sometimes it's a mixture of both, invoking Dolly Parton's "Steel Magnolias" line: "laughter through tears is my favorite emotion."

What the pictures don't show, though, is how soft Lucy's ears were, or how deep her green eyes saw into me. I suppose that's what memories are for, though. But I worry that in time I will forget the details of living with her.

For now, I keep remembering she's gone, and it feels like it's happened all over again. For instance, the boys leave the door open and I panic thinking she got out. Or, I forget to put the butter away and it's still there when I return. And following meals, crumbs remain on the floor, a job Lucy handled for me.

I opened the trunk to load groceries and found her leash and food dish. I remembered it was there from the last, and final, time I had to coax her into the van after she pulled another in a series of Houndini shenanigans. I sobbed in the parking lot of Fred Meyer.

We have other things to remember her by, the shredded carpet, torn door jamb and missing siding. She wasn't the easiest dog, it's true.

So there are flashes of relief mixed with the grief, because I don't have to worry about her getting out and hurt, or hurting someone else, anymore. But with that comes guilt, and then more grief.

While it is crushing to find her bone hidden in the corner, or to vacuum up the last of her hair and find a new home for her belongings, I know that a few houses away from mine, a mother is having to do that with her baby's things. And the perspective shocks me into lacing my grief with gratitude for what I've had and for what remains.

Keeping the season within realm of reason

DEC 4

Between marital and financial challenges combined with the recent death of our dog, it's been a tough year at our house.

We've somehow managed to stay focused on our blessings as we've made many adjustments and acclimated to a new kind of normal. Still, I'm beyond ready to enter into a season of gratitude and celebration.

I know not all of us share the same faith, but most can agree this is a festive, fun time of year—except when it's overshadowed by an overwhelming sense of time moving too fast to capture it all. I have one single goal this season—savoring it.

When I opened the trunk that once housed my mother's Christmas decorations and now houses mine, I caught a whiff of my childhood. As I pulled out Mom's apron, I was transported to memories of this magical time of year.

Instead of longing for my own childhood, though, I felt thankful for what my parents did to make my memories so special. And I was thrilled with the possibilities for doing the same for my children.

Not one of my fond memories include a specific gift, which is encouraging, considering that in our household, we are still recovering from some financial fiascoes. Christmas doesn't have a price tag, no matter what commercial interests wish for us to think.

Since our culture trains its consumers young, I have turned my sons' desire to have everything under the sun into fun games.

First, while at the store, they take a mental picture and upload it to Santa. This is done easily by focusing on the desired item and blinking quickly while holding a mental image.

At home, I collect catalogs and fliers so the kids can cut out pictures and paste them into a Santa book.

I think it's best to establish realistic expectations early on.

When Sam asked for a new puppy, my heart sank. The answer was no, but I made a mental note that the next answer would be yes, even if he asked for—heaven forbid—a skateboard.

I regretted that as soon as I heard him say, "and a sister."

While you're addressing expectations for the kiddos, don't forget to address your own. For instance, does everything have to be perfect? Does everyone have to be on board? Or, can you consider creating your own joy, and therefore the children's own?

Not everyone has a partner who embraces the holidays equally and enthusiastically. But that doesn't need to sideline everyone else for the season.

My husband is a good sport about festivities, but he can take or leave most of them. So I just pick a handful of favorites for the entire family.

One way to savor the season is to make a bucket list of things you'd love to do. Ask members of your family to write their own and then compare lists.

My list is long, so it helps to keep in mind that while I can do some of the things, I can't do all of the things.

I combined my list with those of my kids and picked a few to focus on. For instance, while many people love to schlep into the woods to cut their own Christmas tree, I prefer to have mine delivered by my husband, who has the boys help sneak it into the house.

That presents me with a double surprise—a nice tree and everyone dry, warm and clean.

As I sift through the trunk mixed with decorations from Slovakia and Target, memories of my childhood mix with those of my present, and I am reminded that childhood doesn't keep.

I treasure the keepsakes in my trunk and am glad for the opportunity to cultivate happiness in myself and my kids. To teach the boys that by example is as good a gift as any I could wrap.

No snow? No problem. Surprise little ones by raiding the recycling bin and wadding up enough paper to cover the living room floor. When the snowball fight is finished, back to the bin it goes.

Have fun with food. A shake of sprinkles makes a plain bowl of oatmeal special. Cookie cutters make toast and sandwiches festive. A candy cane makes a perfect stirring stick.

Put on pajamas and have a popcorn party while watching a favorite Christmas movie

Consider bringing your own Elf on the Shelf home for a month of elfish antics for the kids. Learn more at www.elfontheshelf.com.

Collect 25 Christmas books from local book stores, secondhand stores, garage sales and your attic. Wrap them all up and read a new one every night until Christmas.

Meaningful action starts with silence

JAN 8

Two weeks before Christmas, a shopping mall, a kindergarten classroom, a hospital and a freeway were all scenes of random shooting sprees where lone armed gunmen killed innocent victims, leaving behind a wake of shock, grief and fear.

As I watched the Sandy Hook school shooting story unfold, I was brought back to a September morning one month after our wedding. As my husband and I dressed for work in our tiny apartment, we watched in stunned silence as the second of the World Trade Center towers fell.

In the days following September 11, I struggled to draw a full breath as I waited, chest tight, for the other shoe to drop.

What was happening? What would happen next? Where could I hide?

As the concept of terrorism made its way back into our national discourse and collective consciousness, we saw a quick response in changes to airport security. Following the arrest of one wannabe shoe bomber, we now take our shoes off and accept long lines at the airport.

I wonder what our collective, personal and political response will be in response to this recent rash of a different kind of terrorism. This kind of terrorism has the potential of robbing us of joy and peace of mind as we are reminded that nothing is sacred and no place offers safe harbor from harm.

I was back to asking myself the same questions: What was happening? What would happen next? Where can I hide?

Like many parents, for days following the tragedy in Sandy Hook, I couldn't hold my kids tightly enough. However, they didn't understand my desperate desire to cling to them, and wriggled out of my prolonged hugs to run off and play.

So I revised my strategy and gave in to their oft-refused requests to snuggle all night long. I wanted to hold them forever.

But I found myself waking up cranky with a cricked neck because, as anyone who has spent the night dodging elbows to the eye and feet to the ribcage knows, it might sound sweet, but there's nothing restful about it.

You know what else isn't restful? Mentally wandering through all the worse-case scenarios and knowing that there isn't anything that can be done to stop the dark from falling.

That's actually good news, because instead of trying to predict and prevent madness, I can focus my energy on creating the kind of world I do want to live in. I can also continue my efforts to instill the types of values I want my boys to embrace, primarily by example.

The truth is, in addition to worrying about what might happen to them, I also worry how to make sure my kids don't become the perpetrators of such heinous acts.

It is time, way past time, for a respectful, honest conversation about gun control and mental health, and the rights of all over the rights of some. But, myself included, it is nearly impossible to have such a discourse when we aren't listening for anything other than agreement with our own passionate arguments.

One of the first things I think needs to happen in response to this unleashing of hatred is a national conversation about what's really at the root of it.

My bet is that it's not any single thing, but rather some big things we aren't addressing in a meaningful fashion. Facebook status updates aside, what are we really doing to stop the madness?

Bottom line, I think we must start this conversation differently than we usually do: silently.

From my initial response and comments I'm hearing and seeing, it seems we're coming from a reactive place of fear instead of a reflective position of understanding.

Mental illness and how we deal with it, or don't, is something we need to be talking about. Unfortunately, we're eager to sweep that subject under the rug or, we talk about it in low, hushed voices.

Mental illness is an issue we need to put more of an investment into studying, treating and funding. Period.

As for the gun control conversation: could the extreme sides of the issue please stand down already? In what reality will we be able to eradicate all guns? Do we really want only the craftiest of criminals to have them?

And, on the extreme other side of the debate are those advocating for all to be armed. Really? Perhaps I should start packing pistols in the boys' lunch pails. Middle ground, people. We need to find it.

But we can't until we start naming the values we agree on. For instance, those who want a gun in every teacher's waistband and those who want to eradicate them entirely have something critical in common: a desperate desire to protect children.

Before we can tackle these big issues, I think we need to look at how we foster connection and our sense of community. What do we have in common, and how can we build on that?

I submit that at the root of our collective chaos is spiritual bankruptcy. By which I don't mean we all have to recite the same prayer at the table, but how many of us are even sitting at a table to eat with other people? How many of us say any kind of grateful blessing before meals, or ever? How many people are completely isolated, left to fend for themselves and feeling no connection with others, much less something bigger than ourselves?

To accomplish that, we must stop pretending to have all the answers. We have to stop laying the burden of blame on every obvious target. We must, instead, look within to contribute to changing our culture from one of entitlement to one embracing gratitude and life itself.

Food for thought

FEB 5

If it's true that we are what we eat, then our consumer culture must think children are crap.

If you think that's harsh or overly dramatic, stroll the aisles of grocery stores to see what is marketed to children and parents as "kid food." Frankly, I think the food kids eat is directly related to the health and behavior problems we're witnessing in epidemic numbers across the country.

Seeing these bright packages containing equally bright and therefore artificially colored foods makes me crazy. Seeing carts pushed by well-meaning parents stocked with boxes of this kind of fake food makes me cringe.

I don't cringe, mind you, in judgment of the parents, rather in reflection of their lack of knowledge about what is actually inside those boxes. They're designed to make life easier when it's really not that hard to cook healthy in the first place.

It's just that we've bought into the myth that there is a certain type of food for kids and cooking for them is somehow different than cooking for ourselves.

I used to make all of my boys' baby food. And I recently learned just how easy it is to make applesauce instead of buying overpriced jars of the commercial kind at the store.

For those with little ones just beginning to transition to solid food, I caution against buying into the kid food culture. I know that what I did with my two kids worked, despite warnings, admonishments and raised eyebrows from others.

I have plenty of parenting failures to share, and have done so over the years. But one of our success stories happens to be how we deal with food at home.

I'm happy to share those specifics with anyone who asks, but for the purpose of this column, I'll just say the conscious choices I made required thinking beyond "kid food." And my kids are healthier for it.

They are also empowered to make healthy choices going forward, because I have taught them why we need to fuel our bodies in a certain way. For example, even at 5, Sam knows his protein sources like he knows his colors.

We talk in terms of properly fueling our bodies with water and food to avoid making eating about power and control, and therefore a struggle.

When we're at the store and the kids ask for something on the shelf, say a box of really tasty looking bright pink frosted cookies, I cheerfully pull it off the shelf and read the ingredients out loud. I don't usually have to go too far before Sam says it doesn't sound very good.

When it comes to food packaged in the form of their favorite characters like Lightning McQueen, I ask them how they feel about being tricked into wanting things that are bad for them. "That's rude!" Sam says.

This next thing freaks people out, but I've also taught them to examine other, um, clues from their bodies about what they need more, or less, of in their diets.

Sure, it's a little awkward in public bathrooms, when Sam announces he needs to drink more water because his pee is too yellow, or that he needs more fiber because his poop didn't float. I figure, when you have little kids you end up talking more about poop than you ever dreamed possible, so might as well make it educational.

One of the first experiences I had in validation of my commitment to the boys' nutrition was when I gave in to letting Sam have little lollipops and M&Ms as potty training bribes. He nearly always chose his favorite color, red.

About the same time, my mostly sweet boy started throwing terrifying tantrums. As in, "maybe we should take him to the emergency room" scary.

While some observers suggested a spanking was in order, I knew it wasn't just a behavioral issue. After doing some research, I came to learn consuming red dye can trigger a physical reaction that manifests itself in a child going completely out of control.

No, I don't have an official doctor's diagnosis. I don't need one. After all, it's my kid.

And guess what? Since we pulled red dye out of his diet, he hasn't had an episode like that.

It's shocking to see how much red dye a kid can consume, because it's in so many things, from M&Ms to ketchup to chocolate pudding to children's medicine. That's why reading labels is an absolutely critical part of looking out for kids' nutritional welfare.

Sam knows he can't have red dye because it's not good for him. He gets it. So he monitors himself.

He's allowed to have as much of "God's red" as he wants. So if God grew it, we're good with it.

That covers strawberries, cherries, raspberries, apples, beets and watermelon. But for some reason, that little boy wouldn't care if God personally handed him a tomato; he wants nothing to do with those.

I'm not smug about any of this. I know eating broccoli and tofu now doesn't mean my boys won't try to live on Red Bull and Doritos in college.

But I'll sleep a bit more soundly knowing I did my best to make sure they know better.

Beware the bully label

MAR 5

The other day as we were driving home, apropos of nothing, my 5-year-old son said, "Mama, when you yell at me, or use your mean voice, it doesn't show me that you love me."

That statement made me grateful I hadn't ever received one of those proverbial mother-of-the-year awards, because it would no doubt have been revoked in some awkward fashion.

He kept looking out the window, so it was hard to read his face in the rearview mirror.

"What makes you say that?" I asked, taking a deep breath to avoid trying to justify myself or dismissing his feelings just because they made me feel like a jerk.

"I don't want you to be a bully," he said.

I took another deep breath, then asked him to tell me what he thought a bully was.

"When someone is mean, or when they don't want to play with you, or when you say I can't play a game on your phone," he said.

"Yeah, dat is mean," piped up my 3-year-old from his side of the backseat.

I've been bullied myself, and I mean the kind involving spitting, name-calling and clothes-ripping attacks triggering nightmares. I actually tried to kill myself because of it in seventh grade, so I'm all for calling out bullies.

However, in order to best combat bullying, we have to define it clearly. We must guard against watering down our definition to the point it is meaningless.

Bullying is the use of force or coercion to abuse or intimidate others. Often habitual, it may be facilitated by an imbalance in social or physical power.

Setting limits on screen time doesn't fit the bill. Not by a long shot.

I took the opportunity to tell the boys that if someone is making them feel bad, they need to look at the situation and see what they can do differently.

I know some people would call that blaming the victim. But as an advocate for victims of domestic violence, I don't buy that.

Blaming the victim is asking a rape victim what she was wearing. Asking my son to consider his own role in his suffering is essential to his ability to change it, though that's not something I understood myself at the time.

Even after my family moved, enabling me to leave the worst of the bullying behind me, I'd still face situations that sent me home in tears. And each time, my dad would ask me what I did to contribute to the problem.

"You never take my side!" I would cry. "You don't love me!"

But the opposite was true, I realize now. He loved me enough to teach me that in every encounter, we play a role. If we can look back and learn from exchanges we don't like, we can handle them differently next time.

So I think, as important as it is to have conversations about bullying, we need to be aiming to raise resilient children capable of sticking up for themselves and for each other.

I know the damage bullying can do. I still hear the echoes of young voices taunting me. But I now have the perspective of distance to know what I could have been done differently in dealing with those encounters.

Those are lessons I'd like to leave with my boys, who, by the way, seem to have forgiven me for the aforementioned yelling.

Sam, who appears to do his best thinking in the car, described an interaction he had with another boy. "You tell me to look at other people to see how they are feeling," he said, but this boy "didn't even notice I was making a face to show I was mad."

"Not everyone has learned to watch other people for cues about feelings," I said. "Well, I wish everyone had you for a mom," Sam responded.

Who knows? Maybe I'm still in the running for that coveted award after all.

Fair expectations and other failures

APR 9

My sons can switch from fits of laughter to fisticuffs in a matter of minutes over who gets to play with the green train, who owns the brown stegosaurus, who gets which side in the car and who gets unbuckled first. All that is to say, anything is fair game for a fight between my 3- and 5-year-olds.

And while they're not exactly Cain and Abel, Sam and Jake's sibling rivalry, albeit an apparently earnest pursuit of the elusive expectation of fairness, was starting to make me crazy. That is, until I realized a tool as simple and neutral as a calendar could end a substantial amount of the bickering.

Now, when they start the shenanigans, I simply point out which day of the month it is. If it's an even-numbered day, Jake, who was born on the 14th of January, gets to decide who climbs into the van first to sit where. If it's an odd-numbered day, Sam, who was born on the 7th of October, can choose which television show they get to watch when.

The odds and evens system is working so well, I should get some sort of peace prize for thinking of it. But perhaps that's reserved for those who figure out how to handle the fights my system doesn't resolve.

Those are the ones that fall under what I call the fairness factor, something children seem to be keenly in touch with. I swear, my two seem to look for reasons to be slighted.

"How come Jake's heart is bigger than my heart?" Sam asked after seeing two lunch sacks on the counter.

I responded, "Or, you could say: 'Thanks, Mom, for getting up early and making sure I know you love me at lunchtime.'"

And he responded, "Are you being sarcastic? His heart is really bigger than mine."

Yes, it was. The heart I drew in blue, Jake's favorite color, was indeed a smidge bigger than the one I drew in red for Sam. But that smidge was big enough to send Sam storming away upset at the unfairness of it all.

Where do kids get the idea that everything should always be fair in the first place? Oh, right. They get it from us.

I spent a week conducting an experiment where I listened to conversations with an ear for how often the idea of fairness came up. I was amazed to see how much misery we experience by the expectation of fairness even though my friends and I were raised with the expression, "Life's not fair."

Although I tell my kids, "Life's not fair," I'd been acting as if it should be. And that sent a different message.

For instance, I had been carefully measuring their portions, even counting the number of grapes on each plate, to keep things fair and even. Then I realized I was doing them no favors by setting them up to believe everything should be fair.

In truth, some things in life are just unfair. The people who achieve the most success are the ones who've stopped taking that personally and embraced it a fact of life.

Instead of protecting my kids from that fact, I am now focused on raising them to learn how to deal with disappointments and both real and perceived injustices. I am focused on getting them to jump to positive conclusions instead of taking everything so personally.

Of course, that whole leading by example thing comes up here, as it does in all aspects of parenting. So I'm monitoring my own tendency to look for the fairness factor in my daily dealings.

It's really hard to watch your kid's face fall when he's disappointed. However, tempting as it is to step in and try to regulate the situation, I've been resisting the urge. I've come to understand that learning how to fail with grace is something we also need to master.

A common maxim for parents is, "Pick your battles." And I think that applies to children as well.

If we let our kids deal with their own battles, while we're standing by to support them, they will have far less to fight about when we're no longer hovering nearby.

Mostly making the most of it

MAY 10

When I was brand new at this whole mothering gig, the advice "it goes so fast, cherish every minute" used to sound like an admonishment. If I was feeling particularly hostile, it sounded like an accusation.

Of course, as those words washed over me, I might well have been covered in some sort of smelly fluid and extremely sleep deprived. Such is mothering.

Contrary to even my own pre-partum expectations, I was most certainly not enjoying every single minute of motherhood, and I was angry at having something else to add to my list of things to feel guilty about.

Half a decade and two kids later, I'm thinking I over-reacted to strangers who encouraged me to keep in mind what matters most. Of course, I'm getting more sleep these days, and that may be directly proportional to my improved state of mind.

Still, as my friends are having brand new babies and lamenting the lost sleep and all the ways a tiny, little person can make simple things like showering and running an errand difficult, I'm surprised to catch that same advice on the tip of my tongue.

I've decided to modify the aforementioned message by taking a page out of the French writer Voltaire's book. As he advised, don't let the perfect be the enemy of the good.

If we can strive to enjoy most of the moments most of the time, I'd say we have the makings of a pretty happy life.

Of course, while the days of sweeping up Cheerios and changing diapers every time I turn around are behind me, I'm still stepping on Legos and slipping on Matchbox cars. So I might still be too close to the action to have much perspective.

Even this close to the starting line, I'm already finding I've forgotten how hard it was in those early days. Instead, I feel myself longing for some of those sweet moments I remember, even if I didn't exactly cherish them at the time.

That actually gives me hope that my kids will cherry-pick their childhood memories—hope they will mostly remember me the way I want them to instead of as the mom who lost her patience at the first hint of whining.

I can honestly say I've come to accept motherhood as a seesaw of awesome and awful—all day, every day. That's just how it is, because instead of a television show featuring caricatures of people, I am parenting in real life with no commercial breaks.

Even when parenting doesn't go from awesome to awful in the time it takes to turn your back, you're still dealing with human beings, not puppets. So things can go sideways with no warning, and often do.

For example, we're almost out the door. Everybody is clean, dressed and fed. Except Jake has no shoes.

He wants to wear his red boots. And not his red rubber boots, his red cowboy boots. So now there are tears.

This gives Sam time to remember he wanted to bring his special Lego guy to show his friends. It isn't easy to locate, as it looks as if someone broke into our house and trashed the playroom overnight. So now there are more tears.

They eventually dry up, thanks to the fact we eventually found the right red boots and Sam decided he could bring something else along.

As I catch them in the rearview mirror, singing along to the Imagination Movers, I think this is a pretty good gig after all.

And so it goes. Every. Single. Day.

Except now, I can say I enjoy most of it. Most of the time. And that's good enough for us.

Unpacked baggage

JUN 4

My parents recently moved to California to be closer to me.

Compared to Florida, their immediately previous home, or Slovakia, their original home, it's true. However, visiting Omama and Opapa still involves traveling with two energetic little boys who struggle to sit still for story time, let alone a long flight south.

Add that to all the logistics of traveling with little kids, and my chest filled with anxiety when my parents invited us down for a visit. But they are planning to be out of the country until late fall, so we had to seize this window.

They aren't terribly sympathetic to my traveling concerns. They remember flying overseas with me before the advent of disposable diapers.

Because I want to see them as much as possible, because I know time is promised to no one, and because they offered to foot the bill, we soon found ourselves California-bound.

My dad booked a red-eye. He assured me the boys and I would be able to sleep all the way.

After all, he said, that's what he remembered about me. Of course, he neglected to mention the pacifier dipped in honey and cognac.

I considered packing some cognac for myself, but settled for deep breaths, instead. That, and Dollar Store bribes.

Pack light, my parents advised. I promised I would.

I used to show up with a van-load of gear: highchairs, bibs, baby food, a playpen, a stroller and even an inflatable bath duck. So for me, just lugging a car seat, an enormous, over-stuffed suitcase and a carry-on with some snacks and changes of clothes seemed reasonable.

At least it did as I pulled out of the driveway at 3:30 a.m., patting myself on the back for packing so light. But when we got to the economy parking lot at the airport and realized I had to get all of that, plus two rummy but excited pint-sized travelers to the airport, I got a little short of breath.

Contrary to the stranger danger lesson I am supposed to be instilling in the boys, we learned about the kindness of strangers as people went out of their way to help us. And it became quite necessary, as Jake decided he didn't want to board a shuttle, no matter what.

The trip home was a little different. We couldn't get seats together, and no one was willing to switch.

On the bright side, that took me off the hook for making the boys behave. I don't think the guy in front of Jake appreciated Jake's fascination with the tray attached to the seat, all the way from Palm Springs to Portland.

Meanwhile, Sam spilled his orange juice—twice. So despite the admonishments I got for overpacking, I was glad I had extra clothes on board.

For the record, none of us slept.

The visit itself was as much as an adventure as the traveling.

My parents and I have different opinions on—well, maybe it's easier to just tell you what we have in common, which is love and affection for each other.

On our last visit, I made the mistake of taking my mom's rules for the kids, drastically different from mine, as a personal commentary on my parenting.

This time, I asked her what the rules were up front, then set the stage with the boys so she didn't have to admonish them all weekend for making every flat surface a race track.

Now that we've established that our different approaches to parenting don't constitute a reflection on each other's, we've dropped our defenses and can actually learn from each other.

I bought Jake some water wings. My mom said I paid too much for them and should return them.

I said I paid more because fabric wings were better. But I was wrong.

It took two of us to wrestle them onto Jake's little arms, and the fabric tore within hours.

My dad pointed out another problem. He thought Jake was getting too confident in the water—more so than was warranted.

A sudden splash behind us illustrated his point, as Jake jumped in, sans wings, forcing me to dive in after him, fully clothed.

But the lessons went both ways.

When Jake and I wrapped up a prolonged session of him working through the disappointment of making a bad decision, my mom said she admired my patience. She said she liked how I let him experience the consequences and express his feelings without mine getting in the way.

"I didn't have that kind of patience," she admitted. "You had lots of other things," I responded.

And she did, not the least of which was a way of cooking food that made you feel her love.

When she asked Sam during breakfast what he wanted for dinner, he said he couldn't choose.

"It's too hard to choose, Omama. Everything you cook is so good," Sam said, eating a third helping of palacinky.

On the way home from the airport, Sam announced he was planning to move to California when he grew up so he could be closer to Omama and Opapa. Also, because it's sunny there all the time.

Fine, I said.

I look forward to hearing about his adventures traveling with small children to visit me. If he packs an inflatable duck, I will say nothing. I might, however, remind him to pack an extra change of clothes and use lidded cups.

I got a letter the other day from my mom. Enclosed was a receipt for the water wings, which she had returned.

Turns out she was right about that, too.

For the love of Squinkies

JUL 16

Something I didn't even know was a word became the bane of my mothering when my 5-year-old happened to ask if he could have a Squinky.

Is that even English? I wondered.

It sure is. And given the squishy nature of Squinkies, they're not as painful to step on as Legos.

But they come with other complications, such as being extremely habit-forming. Think crack for kids.

Apparently the tiny, squishy rubber toys, which come packaged in teeny plastic bubbles, first became a hit in 2010.

And while it's a mystery for some how the Squinky phenomenon caught fire, that's easy for me. After dealing with complex inquiries all day, it's nice to get a simple one lobbed your way.

So you say yes. Yes, Sam, you can have a Squinky.

Except, it turns out, there's really no such thing as "a" Squinky.

These little choking hazards, shaped in the likeness of small animals or popular children's characters, come in sets. It turns out Squinkies, dear readers, are collectibles.

That's exactly what toymaker Bill Nichols had in mind when his company, Blip Toys, a 16-person operation based in Minnetonka, Minn., came out with these little landfill-destinees. "With one purchase, the child will become an instant collector," he announced at the time.

But it seemed to me that Sam became more than simply a Squinky enthusiast. He became more like a crack addict desperate for just one more fix.

With fond memories of my own childhood collections, I aided and abetted Sam as he began to amass his collection.

Alas, as with most aspects of parenting, nothing is as simple as it seems.

What do the Squinkies do, anyway, the non owner might ask. Well, nothing, actually.

Of course, the mermaids and Strawberry Shortcake dolls of my childhood didn't do anything either. My imagination did the work.

That's the point. That's the beauty of it.

Kids use their imagination in playing with them. I love seeing that, though I'm surprised at the things they come up with.

For instance, Sam would like to start making videos capturing his thoughts on Squinkies, such as how the excess packaging (too much garbage, he says) and how easily the paint comes off (very easily if you put them in your mouth, he notes).

I plan to make a cameo appearance in his video to point out that manufacture's recommendations and mom's rules recommend against putting them in your mouth.

My rough-and-tumble boys are so tender with these teensy toys. As bizarre as the trend seems to me, I can't deny they love them.

In fact, when Sam lost his little Star Wars figure, he shed more tears than I did when my wedding ring went missing.

"It's the droid you've been looking for!" I said when I finally found it outside, under a dandelion leaf. But, it seemed he was too excited to be reunited with "Darf Vader" to get it.

Early on, I made a tactical error and bought some on sale in advance. Suddenly I had a willing, albeit annoying, helper.

At every turn, Sam stood at the ready to earn another Squinky. Sorting socks, check. Watering plants, sweeping stairs, check. If there was a Squinky to be earned, the kid was on it.

It was fun at first, going with Sam to find new Squinkies. I remember how special it made me feel when my mom bought me something special, like plastic charms for my charm bracelet.

But now Sam is waking up and coming downstairs already dressed, and picking up things that aren't even his, without being asked, in hopes of earning another Squinky.

That raised a concern with me. I didn't want him thinking every good deed had to be rewarded by a material thing. I stressed to him that he should do the right thing simply because that's part of being a decent human being.

Then he asked if he could use some of his own money to buy his brother a special set of Squinkies, after having priced them at three different stores. And I thought, maybe I don't have to worry so much about the good human being lesson.

As I got ready for work this morning, I wondered if I could honestly say the Squinky hassle is worth it.

When I walked back in the door, the boys were hugging. Jake was excited, eager to show me a tiny tow-truck Squinky he'd been searching for.

"Look, Mom, it's the droid he was looking for!" Sam said, beaming.

Looks like maybe the kid gets it after all.

Lessons from the field

JUL 12

I admire people who live off the land. Sometimes I think I'd like to be one of them.

The truth is, I'd be all over it if it weren't for all the hard and often dirty work involved. Instead, I tend to buy my food from other actual hard-working people—or at Safeway.

Every summer, one of my best friends goes to pick various kinds of berries and invites me along.

"It's fun!" she says. After the inevitable pause, she adds, "And rewarding!"

That's where I usually zone out. Rewarding and work aren't two words I like to combine on weekends.

When I drive by fields where people are working, it doesn't strike me as particularly recreational. It looks like hard, uncomfortable work. So why would I want to do that for "fun"?

But I finally gave in. And now I can say that while it's not the same sort of fun as, say, reading poolside with an umbrella in my drink, I did find something deeply satisfying in my recent foray into the strawberry fields.

It made for a dirty, but also delightful and delicious, morning. And that's despite the fact we had three young children to keep an eye on.

Fortunately, when it involves sweet berries, kids can be surprisingly industrious. When they got distracted, the wide-open field was a bonus.

My 5-year-old, Sam, impressed me with his determination to get the most berries in his bucket.

First, he learned that the closer he worked to the thistles, the more berries he found. "It must be because people don't like to get poked," he reasoned.

I agreed, but from a distance, as I was one of the people avoiding his "no pain no gain" line of reasoning.

Jake, 3, was more like me. He took a more, shall we say, laid back approach. His methodology was more along the lines of, "one for the bucket, one for me; one for the bucket, one for me." When his bucket was empty, that changed to "another one for me" out of his brother's bucket.

Sam solved that problem, and improved his efficiency, by sitting on his bucket, open side up. "This way I can pick and drop, pick and drop, so I can get more berries and Jake can't have any of mine," he said.

After we got home, stained with berry juice and some blood, as Sam's thistle theory was spot on, we mixed all of our berries together and embarked on a jam-making exercise. That also falls into the "rewarding work" category, by the way.

Making strawberry jam was messy, time consuming, a little dangerous and, frankly, still a whole lot of fun.

The day ended up being totally dedicated to the adventure of picking, freezing and jam-making. Some would consider it the waste of a perfectly good Saturday, but not me—not now that I've edged a few steps closer to embracing the living off the land thing.

I'm not committing myself to moving into the wilderness and relying on my homesteading skills, of course. In that scenario, I would perish.

However, I am eager to commit to more adventures like this, where we get a little dirt under our nails while learning more about preserving fruit and the planet.

While it would be much faster to just buy berries and berry jam, I enjoy the fruits of our labor, so to speak, every morning when I spread our homemade jam on toast or sandwiches, or just sneak a spoonful.

Inspired by a friend, I started to analyze the economics by calculating the cost of the berries, the hours of picking time, the drive to and from and the time, supplies and equipment going into the jam-making part of the exercise. I figured I'd have to include the cost of the jars and tools needed to avoid third-degree burns.

But how does buying a box of berries or jar of jam at Safeway compare, from a psychic rewards point of view, to picking your own berries in the field and making your own jam in the kitchen? It's not even close.

Sometimes the values of living what I like to think of as a homemade life extend beyond the reach of calculators and checkbooks.

I can't attach a price to the value of watching my kids learn first-hand what it is that we're actually trying to protect with all the recycling, errand-clustering and water-conserving we do at home. I think having that experience of harvesting something from the soil makes the green living messages more meaningful, thus more sustainable.

And turning that harvest into something we can savor long after the berry stains come out of our clothes—they will come out, right?—leaves a lingering reminder of why it matters.

Confessions of a reforming yeller

AUG 9

I have a confession to make. Even though I love my boys to the moon and back, I yell at them. Not just once in a blue one either. I don't want to admit this to myself, much less to you, but it's more like all the time.

Well, maybe not all the time. But it may feel like it could be any time to my boys, ages 3 and 5.

I actually didn't realize how often I was doing it until I consciously tried to stop.

I signed on to take what's called The Orange Rhino Challenge, laid down by a woman in the blogosphere who found herself in a similar situation.

I make a concerted effort to parent intentionally, which is to say I put a lot of thought into the things I do and why I do them.

For instance, I don't really spank my boys, because I'm not one of those people who can do it calmly after counting to 10 or whatever.

The few times I spanked them, it felt more like hitting someone in anger. It just didn't feel right. Besides, if I have the presence of mind to count calmly to 10, I can usually figure out another way to deal with the issue at hand without using mine.

It turns out I'm in good company, as the New York *Times* ran an article a few years ago called "For Some Parents, Shouting is the New Spanking."

Recently I yelled at my oldest to quit screwing around at 10 p.m. because that was the only time I had to myself all weekend and I really wanted to get some writing done. But it sounded harsher in real life than it does here on paper.

Sam did that thing where he flinches at the sound of my voice rising, and I realized it wasn't even him I was mad at. I sensed the injustice he must feel when he's just being a 5-year-old and gets reamed out instead of simply being corrected, with a logical consequence attached to misbehavior.

"I just want you to snuggle me, Mama," he said. There were tears, his followed by mine.

So, we snuggled. And I apologized for yelling and told him I would work on that.

As I snuggled with him I wondered: What if I'm just a yeller? Maybe that's just the deal and we can laugh about it later like my mom and I laugh about her "flying hand."

But right now, it's not funny. Right now I have a little boy who doesn't deserve getting yelled at even if, or perhaps especially if, he's pushing my buttons.

Logically I know I can do better than shouting, but it seems to be my default mode. What if I can't change?

Those were some of my thoughts as I prayed about the situation. Then I stumbled upon The Orange Rhino website and learned about the no-yelling-for-365-days challenge.

In it's most basic form, it's like this: If you yell, you have to return to day one and start over. I have yelled so loud, my throat hurt. Recently, in fact.

Sometimes it's HEY! Yelled from across the room or the front seat of the car.

Sometimes it's GET IN THE CAR NOW, ensuring we get the day off to a cheerful start. Sometimes it's GO TO SLEEP, because that's as relaxing as any lullaby. But always, it makes me feel like a jerk. And always, it makes me wish I hadn't.

With the Orange Rhino challenge, I started off with five days on the calendar marked in orange. Some would say that's not much to be proud of, as I shouldn't be shouting at small children in the first place. They may or may not have small children who display insanely impulsive behavior at totally inconvenient times. Either way, I don't worry much anymore what Those People think.

What I'm more concerned about is making personal changes that create a happier home. What I am proud of is that my boys will always know it's OK to make mistakes as long as they keep learning from them.

They will know that because they watch me do it every day.

By the way, I had to start over again. But I'm back to three days in a row of no shouting.

This morning, I told my youngest he was my favorite 3-year-old on all the planet. He said I was his favorite mommy, but couldn't resist adding:

"I don't like it when you yell like a T-Rex, Mama. But you are being a good triceratops."

Jake insists Rudolph is a cow rather than reindeer and a rhinoceros is a dinosaur. But I get his point.

Turns out being a soccer mom is a team sport

SEP 6

It took me nearly six years to get here, but judging by my calendar, and the clutter in my car, it seems I've rounded a corner. It seems my minivan and I are now headed toward some new adventures in motherhood.

Let me give you a hint. It involves cleats, shin guards and Saturday mornings spent on muddy sidelines.

Yes, I've finally arrived. I'm officially a soccer mom.

And while "soccer mom" is an expression that vexes some, I've been looking forward to it. That's because I'm okay with being in a box so long as I'm the one who checks it.

Say I were standing in the lobby of life when someone handed me a clipboard and said, "Check all that apply." I could check daughter, wife, mother, friend, sister, woman and writer.

Now, let's say under each of those featured a series of subcategories with adjectives modifying each role. I could cheerfully check the box identifying me as a mom who is enthusiastic about supporting her kids' activity of choice. And please note the singular use of the word "activity."

Of course, my initiation into being a soccer mom didn't exactly match the vision in my head.

For starters, we kicked off Sam's athletic career by missing his first practice. It seems I missed the message telling me that practice was starting the next day.

That message continued on to note he would have games every Saturday for the next few months, along with two practices a week, starting at the same time I typically get off work.

Which brings me to the next unexpected element of being a soccer mom: At our house, it's a team sport—a relay race, if you will—to get the kid on the field on time.

When I imagined what motherhood would be like, I was missing a few things, including a kid and a crystal ball.

What I didn't know was that I wouldn't be home with the boys any more by the time they were this age. So I wasn't expecting being a soccer mom to include letting their dad be their dad.

When I stayed home with the boys, all things kid-related fell under my umbrella. I sometimes forget there are two of us holding the umbrella now. I always pictured my husband at the games, and kicking the ball around the backyard, but I didn't factor him into the other logistics.

When I launched into a freak-out session about how Sam was going to get to practice, when I would still be at work, my husband calmly suggested he take on that responsibility. In fact, he said he'd be happy to.

But, I still play a key role—making sure the shin guards, cleats, socks and shorts are packed, along with a snack and water bottle.

I had some of that stuff ready to go by the second practice. I say some, because while practice was starting I was still parked on Highway 99W in Dundee, ripping the packaging off the special soccer socks I'd completely forgotten about until my lunch break.

When I made it to the field, I noticed Sam didn't have any water in his water bottle.

Sam shrugged. "You forgot to put water in it, Mom."

I pointed out that, like Jesus, I preferred to help those who helped themselves. I also noted this was my first time having a kid in sports.

"You're doing pretty good," he said, before grabbing his soccer ball.

I'd meant to write his name on it with a permanent marker. But on closer inspection, I saw it was already labeled in my husband's familiar handwriting.

The guy's doing pretty good, too.

Whereas I once slept through Saturday mornings entirely, I am now on the sidelines with my husband, cheering on the kid in the orange cleats.

Sam said he picked them because they were my favorite color. But mostly, it was because we waited until the last minute, and there wasn't much to choose from that fit.

Minivan, check. Soccer gear, check. I guess now all that I'm missing is the stick figure family decal for my back window.

I do, however, have mud-flap style stickers of a pony-tailed girl reading, which tells people that I also fall into the box of "reader." And I can also check these subcategories: avid reader, poly-reader and the kind of reader who writes in the margins.

Please, don't excuse the mess

SEP 20

I'm not going to write about how to clean your house, because that would be both hypocritical and hysterical. Instead, I'm going to focus on why it matters, while begging you to stop apologizing for putting it off.

Perhaps the most common expression houseguests get is, "Please excuse the mess."

It's often said by me and people like me. After all, it would take me hours of cleaning, with my children tied to chairs, to even get my house to the level of mess others try to excuse.

My really good friends can't be fooled, of course. They know the broom leaning up against the wall next to a little collection of leaves, Legos and leftover noodles was probably propped up there two days ago. But we pretend I was sweeping the place when I was interrupted by a knock at the door.

I have small people living with me. I call them my children.

That means I keep things just sanitary enough to allow them to eat off the floor, as I also follow the five-second rule, if not the 500-second rule. It also means I can't ever quite keep up, because as Phyllis Diller famously said, "Cleaning your house while your kids are still growing is like shoveling the sidewalk before it stops snowing."

Although my home isn't mortifyingly messy, at least most of the time, I still feel compelled to apologize for the mess. That's because it doesn't look quite like any of the pictures in my ironic collection of Good Housekeeping magazines.

But it's my home. That means it's where I gather family, friends or myself at the end of the day.

I want all of us to feel welcome, so I have to have some baseline of cleanliness and order—a personal threshold, if you will.

I like to wake up to a clean kitchen, as long as that doesn't entail mopping the floor. I only mop if I know company is coming.

I wish floors mattered more to me, because shiny floors make for better first impressions.

Luckily, I'm not so worried about first impressions these days. The kind of visitors I get tend to be more impressed by my all-things-teal spray-painting mission than the state of my floors.

I would prefer people feel welcome at my home than marvel over my sparkling windows, and I'm safe there.

For me, sparkling windows is an entirely theoretical consideration. In reality, my glass surfaces will always feature fingerprints, at least they will until someone other than me decides it matters enough to them to whip out the Windex.

I get my inspiration from my little mess-makers extraordinaire. As much as this is my home, it's their home, too, and I want them to grow up with the sense of security that comes from knowing things are being handled.

I think there is immeasurable comfort in a home kept with love. That may include a degree of order, but isn't something I can fully equate with cleanliness.

I make a constant effort to remind myself I am choosing to do certain chores in order to gain something that matters to me. I consciously let certain chores go because they aren't essential to achieving that.

When I'm walking around the house picking up and folding laundry long after everyone else is asleep, I think of my mom doing exactly the same thing when I was little. And I'm thankful for it.

It probably felt unappreciated, of course. As kids, we just took that kind of thing for granted. We assumed everyone had a mom making sure the sock drawer never went empty.

I grew up with a mom who was fastidious about housekeeping. I am clearly less so.

In truth, my kids don't have a full-fledged sock fairy. I keep a sock box in the entryway, and they are welcome to match as many pairs of socks as they like.

My mom wore the same green apron almost every day for 11 months of the year. In December, she swapped it for one featuring a Christmas theme.

She wore them, of course, to protect her clothes. That's probably because she was always cooking something, usually something amazing.

By the way, she took such good care of her things that I still have her Christmas apron.

I, on the other hand, am prone to purchasing new aprons because they were cute, but never actually putting them on. Not only do I not wear the aprons, but I'm pretty sure my kids learned from me how to use their sleeves as napkins.

I own patterns capable of producing perfectly adorable aprons at home, because I want to be that kind of person. But alas, I am not. I am merely a collector of good intentions.

I am constantly confounded by the fact the people in my household want to eat dinner every single night. I don't know how my mom managed that, and it never dawned on me in 37 years to thank her.

That's not to mention all the dusting and other little things that helped make our house feel like home.

As I write this, it occurs to me that the chores I'm doing right now, even when I feel cranky about them, are helping me pay it forward. And I think it's working.

On the drive home the other day, my 5-year-old, Sam, mentioned his stuffed giraffe was a kid now.

"So that means I have to start doing laundry like you," he said. "Because when you love someone you take care of them."

That pretty much sums it up. He feels as if I'm taking care of him like my mom took care of me, even though she's more like an every-hair-in-place Martha Stewart and I'm more like a disheveled Rachael Ray, plus a few pounds and minus a few cooking skills.

Either way, we have our own style of taking care of our people, and that's the point. Next time someone comes to your door, try welcoming them with open arms and no apologies.

If you simply can't manage it, try this suggestion from Diller: When someone comes over unexpectedly, pause, look about perplexed, shake your head sadly and exclaim, "Who could have done this? We have no enemies."

Off to school: Lessons for mom

OCT 4

When most children in Yamhill County went back to school the same day last month, my boys and I had a little misunderstanding that came to light in the minivan as I was dropping them off at day care.

While there were tears shed across the state by little ones reluctant or afraid to go to school, my boys cried because they weren't going.

I thought Sam knew he wasn't starting until later in the week. But when we rolled up to drop the boys off, he cheerfully told his brother, "Goodbye, Jake. I'm going to kindergarten now."

"And so I go, too," Jake said, compounding the misunderstanding. Though Sam was due to start in a few days, Jake still has a way to go before he gets his first-day pictures.

We got that cleared up pretty quickly, but I was reminded of the confusion I had experienced myself the previous week, when I was given an opportunity to practice reacting to misunderstandings at my first event as the parent of a student.

I'd spent a few years working as a grade school secretary, so I thought I knew the drill. Nope.

I was flustered at the front office, as I arrived barely on time, which is to say late. As I fumbled through my purse for my license, I did not make the first impression I'd hoped as the other parents were gathering in the hall to listen to the teacher.

That leads me to yet another point of confusion. In the letter announcing the meeting, I misunderstood "personal time for you and your child to get to know the teacher and classroom" to mean it would be just us. Instead it was us and half the class.

That was fine. It just wasn't what I was expecting.

After recovering from that, I watched the teacher give the kids a tub of toys and a task: help organize the toys. And I noticed him carefully observing the children to get a sense of each of them and how they responded to both the task and one another.

My kid may or may not have impressed me with his leadership. But in short order, those kids had that tub sorted by color and type as the parents set about dropping off supplies.

Unfortunately, the supply adventure also threw me. It was a bit frustrating for this first-time school mom.

Being pro-active, I went online and downloaded a supply list well in advance. And I'm sure it was designated for the 2013-14 school year, as I compulsively verified that.

But after acquiring everything on the list and tucking it into Sam's backpack, we received a letter in the mail with different supply instructions.

That kind of thing can really mess up a person—like, say, me—who is trying to be perfect. I understand in retrospect that was totally unnecessary, but still.

I'm the kind of person who always wants to be prepared.

But one of the first lessons I learned while sending Sam off to school is that it's not about having the right type of glue sticks or about doing everything right. It's actually about learning how to react to being thrown off. It's about learning how to find your balance when the ground below you has become unsteady.

So, while this is my baby's first year of school, it's also my first year with a kid in school. I trust we'll get it figured out in time for graduation.

Oh, and one more thing. When I first heard through a friend that my son's teacher was going to be a man, I was a little thrown off.

My husband was a teacher, I have male friends who are teachers. But somehow, as with nearly everything else about my parenting experience, having a Mr. teacher for Kindergarten didn't match the picture in my head.

Fortunately, Mr. Teacher quickly impressed me with his enthusiasm, empathy, patience and creative problem-solving. And he really won me over when someone asked him if the kids would have recess, and he responded: "When I was a kid, I was a boy and recess saved my life."

That's when I realized it was all going according to plan, even if it wasn't the one I had envisioned.

Message from a trashcan

OCT 11

After sharing my confessions and challenges as I try to lighten my carbon footprint, it's nice to be able to share one of my successes: I've nearly managed to make waste-free lunches a regular part of my kids' routine.

I throw in the "nearly" caveat because we do still have wrappers from bars to contend with before soccer practice. But by and large, we've got the lunch waste thing as licked as the lids on the applesauce cups my boys used to get.

It was by accident I discovered something that used to be a challenge could become commonplace for me.

I was a little earlier than usual picking up my kids from daycare. As I removed their lunch containers from the bin, I wondered why there weren't more empty containers, with so many kids still there.

Ah, yes. Thanks to Lunchables, there really wasn't a need for lunch boxes and other pesky containers.

If you aren't familiar with them, Lunchables are single-use plastic boxes filled with processed food presented in such a way as to be appealing to children and parents alike.

The company programs parents and children to believe there is such a thing as "kid" food as opposed to "people" food. But I beg to differ. Actually, I delineate the two this way: "crap" and "real food."

I wish I were taller when I stand on my soapbox, because I simply can't compete with the commercial programming suggesting we are too busy to make real food for kids who depend on us for nourishment to sustain them through their day of learning, playing and growing. I think people would be less likely to buy into these craftily marketed but false messages if they knew how easy it actually is.

How hard is it to smear peanut butter on a whole grain tortilla and wrap the tortilla around a banana? Follow those three simple steps and —ta-da!—you've made a monkey dog. Or, add a fourth step and cut it into sushi-like slices.

Round out your nutritious homemade meal by filling a muffin container with peas, cherry tomatoes or fancy-sliced carrots. I spend the extra 20 cents to buy bags of these "special carrots" because my boys swear they are "funner to eat," and "funner" is well worth the modest investment.

I usually put in a couple animal cookies or some other fun snack, and I don't make them eat the snack last. First, I'm not there to enforce that; second, as long as they eat what's in the container, or what it takes to satisfy their hunger, they can choose the order.

But if they don't make good choices, which I observe by checking returning boxes for vegetables, I help them by eliminating the treats until they "remember better."

I get that certain things appeal to kids, like compartments. So I used to serve lunch in a six-cup muffin tin.

But this was not a very eco-friendly system for the road, as it was lidless.

So I invested in a couple of thermoses and some containers designed for the purpose of compartmentalizing lunches. I also got some silicone baking cups to create additional compartments, as well as a few small, square containers for dips and things like applesauce. There are many compartmentalized lunch containers on the market. The ones I picked are called Easy Lunchboxes, and they're awesome. Aside from the initial investment, this is as helpful to my pocketbook as it is for the planet. Single-use products are exponentially more expensive than bulk-purchased foods parceled out among little containers.

According to the Environmental Protection Agency, the average American school-age child throws away 67 pounds of lunch waste a year. It doesn't take a math wizard to understand that a small effort to reduce the waste in each kids' lunch box could add up to a significant difference.

The trick to being successful at waste-free lunches is keeping it cool and simple, and thinking of the little things.

Silverware which is easy to find at garage sales, and cloth napkins come in enough different styles that kids' can pick a few favorites. Dishes and laundry are already a regular part of life, so what's a few extra spoons and napkins?

It might be a minor annoyance to add to housework, but think of it this way: It's a minor annoyance that can have a major impact.

After awhile, it just becomes part of the routine. And it sure beats running out of, say, trees or water, which would really be annoying.

Of course, the routine you wind up with might not be the one you imagined.

I bought extra lunch containers, thinking I would prepare lunches in advance. Instead, I seem to be counting on those extras to buy time between cleaning out the van and running the dishwasher, which I suppose could count as an earth-saving measure in itself.

And now, lest you suspect I never step off my soapbox, I will share a story to show that I do, indeed, come down. And most recently, in an extraordinarily embarrassing way. I include it here as a reminder that we're all works in progress.

First, some background:

I have a bad habit of getting my kids out the door with healthy meals while neglecting my own. In an effort to improve, I picked up a couple of GT's Kombucha drinks, which are fermented and feature raw chia.

In retrospect, the labels do clearly say: Perishable. Keep refrigerated. But I tend to read the kids' labels more than my own, as is evidenced by what happened next.

I drank one and forgot to put the other in the fridge. It sat in the car during one hot day, then another. By the time I discovered it, it had rolled under the seat of my mobile office.

I knew I should just open it, pour the juice out and recycle the glass. But, ew.

Instead, when no one was looking, I tossed it into the trash can under my desk, still unopened. A few days later, we were on deadline when something exploded in the newsroom. I thought the roof was going to come down on our heads.

I looked around to figure out what happened, then noticed there was glass around my feet. Also, there was a putrid smell emanating from— under my desk. Also, I was covered in sticky, rank chia slime.

My concerned co-workers, who quickly realized it was a problem unique to me and not a massive catastrophe, came to assist.

"What happened?" asked one of my most environmentally aware colleagues.

As it dawned on me that the glass bottle in my garbage can had exploded, I realized I'd have to confess what I'd done. I think I was forgiven more easily for tossing the drink than for the awful smell it caused.

Either way, lesson learned: Recycle your glass or it might cut you. Or, something like that.

Even holiday moms have their limits

NOV 5

I was recently asked if I was the kind of mom who sews Halloween costumes for her kids.

Though it was asked casually, when over-analyzed, as is my way, the question can pack a punch. To me, it begs the question: what kind of a mom am I, exactly?

I thought back on my miserable, now hilarious, matching family pajama debacle.

No, I am not the kind of mom who sews Halloween costumes—or anything, actually—despite my plans on Pinterest. Quite the opposite, in fact.

Last year, I intended to make Lego costumes for the boys. At the very last minute, I ordered two angry bird costumes, with two-day delivery courtesy of my Amazon Prime membership.

This year, I saved a few bucks by waiting until our choices were limited to the 40-percent off rack at Fred Meyer. My brother and I went as hobos year after year, and we turned out alright, so I don't feel too bad about this.

I've gone on the record as being a "holiday mom," so you'd think I'd bring a little more to the table for Halloween. But I'm just not a ghouls and goblins kind of girl.

At the end of October, I'm still recovering from Sam's birthday festivities. That's because I'm the kind of mom who makes a big deal out of birthdays. My favorites are those of Sam, Jake and baby Jesus.

For the last one, I lean on the traditions established long before it was my job, and joy, to bring the holidays home for my family. But for the first two, I've been creating our own for the last six years and think I've finally got it down.

My goal is this: to celebrate birthdays in such a way that long after I'm gone, and the glitter from birthdays past stops surfacing in random places, my boys will know how glad I am they were born. Of course, that can be accomplished without the balloons and fanfare, but I have fun adding those touches.

Fun, that is, except when it's the day before the party, and I'm still cutting vegetables to make a platter in the likeness of a favorite Teenage

Mutant Ninja Turtle. That proved to be a hit, by the way, but still no match for pizza.

I will admit that my birthday planning is sometimes reminiscent of my labor experience—kind of a pain, but for a good cause.

I also bear in mind the quote often attributed to Maya Angelou, reminding us that people will forget what you said, people will forget what you did, but people will never forget how you made them feel.

So on the birthday eve, I line the hallway and stairs with foam stars leading all the way to the kitchen table, which is set with a collection of birthday-themed books from the library and balloons for decoration.

Next, we have birthday oatmeal, following a super-simple recipe: steel cut oats topped with coconut milk whipped cream and a liberal doses of sprinkles, as it's dye-be-damned for this occasion. That is served with one of those candles with a number on it, which is one of the little details I obsess about dating back to Sam's first birthday.

Six years ago, I didn't know I was going to be a big birthday mom. In lieu of a first birthday party we took Sam to the beach for the weekend and had a lovely time.

Until, on the way home I realized there was no cake, ergo no picture of Sam blowing out a candle in said cake. And I couldn't have that.

At the time, I was even more rabid about nutrition than I am now, and we wouldn't be home in time for me to make any kind of cake. So on the way home, we picked up a small, insanely expensive little cake-like thing and some pricey frosting-like product. Also, a candle molded into the number "1."

I kept Sam up well past his bedtime, but I got the picture I wanted, as well as the motivation to plan ahead better in future years.

I even have a "birthday bag" containing number candles I'm saving from Sam to re-use for Jake. I consider it a small way to pay back the cost of that first cake, the birthday stars, the whipped cream recipe, and the reminders to interview the birthday boy, mark his height in his chart and take a picture of both boys with their favorite "snuggies," a giraffe for Sam and a zebra for Jake.

Then there's the business of parties and gifts.

There's a notion that these things have to cost a lot of money if you want to "do it right." But except for that first cake, none of the aforementioned things cost a lot of money.

We've learned about budgeting. We actually have a "celebrations" envelope used to pay for gifts, parties, pumpkins and such.

That wasn't always the case. We used to put stuff like that on credit cards. In fact, we even charged the babies, because the hospital was calling to collect on them before their little umbilical cords fell off.

These days, though, we're of a mind that the best gift we can give the boys is a sense of security. And that kind of peace of mind comes with being free of debt, which we're working toward.

Part of that is explaining to the boys about why they can't invite everyone they've ever met to the party.

This year I've added two new things to the mix: wrapping every item in his lunch box, just for the delight of it, and thank you notes for gifts.

When Sam handed a friend a painstakingly handwritten thank you, his mom termed it was a lost art.

Well, here's to lost and found, and three cheers to being whatever kind of mom you want to be, so long as you are able to delight in the little things that make it all worth it.

So, I may not be the kind of mom who sews Halloween costumes, let alone Christmas pajamas. But I did just use a Sharpie to turn a mandarin into a lunchbox pumpkin surprise, and I'm sure that counts for some holiday mom props.

Embracing the Elf on the Shelf

DEC 3

Whether you embrace or eschew Elf on the Shelf, the pint-sized phenomenon is here to stay. At least it is in the Hardy household.

It's the time of year when I begin preparing for our special December visitor. It's hard to say who is more excited: me or the boys.

Nope, it's not Santa. And, no it's not Jesus, either. Though we are fans of both those fellows at our house, the first one is a one-day gig and the latter is an everyday presence. The guest I'm talking about is named Finn, of Elf-on-the-Shelf fame. The boys believe he came from the North Pole, but the truth is he followed me home from Target a few years ago.

One of the best purchases I've made as a holiday mom is the $30 investment in the little doll and hardback book relating the story of how Santa's little narc came to be.

Now that I think of it, maybe the whole elf thing was hatched by the NSA to normalize being spied on, but I didn't buy the elf as a behavior modification device. Mostly, I was sold on the elf's spirit of making merry in our home.

I knew the boys would like the elf, but I never dreamed they would literally fall in love with the mischief maker they named Finn. Nor did I expect to find myself cheerfully inventing ideas for the elf to make more work for me, all in the spirit of creating delightful, magical moments for two of my favorite people on the planet.

Our elf arrives right after Thanksgiving bearing cozy new pajamas, cocoa and marshmallows, which are off limits the rest of the year. He also brings new toothbrushes, by the way. No, the elf doesn't have to buy things, obviously. But he does seem to pick up a few of my December errands, transforming things like new toothbrushes into more exciting events than I ever could.

To be honest, in Finn's world, sometimes magical and messy go hand-in-sticky-from-candy-canes-hand. But mostly he does simple little things to make the boys giggle and eagerly anticipate the next day.

For instance, the boys have awakened to find Finn drinking the maple syrup after making pancakes, with sprinkles. Another time, the little rascal took a dry erase marker and drew mustaches and horns on our framed pictures. Since we're book people, on Dec. 1, he delivers a basket of 25 garage-sale purchased books, wrapped up with instructions to open one each bedtime leading up to Christmas Day.

Not everyone is thrilled about the advent of this new tradition. And I get it; really, who wants more messes? But, luckily, the elf is smart enough to use dry-erase markers and seems to be familiar with my personal threshold for messes, so we're good there.

Plus, childhood is the shortest of seasons. What's a few more sprinkles to sweep up in addition to the daily accumulation of crumbs, leaves and dirt?

And to be clear, nowhere in the Elf manual does it suggest the elf should do all that stuff, the aptly named toy is cool with simply sitting on the shelf.

Not all moms embrace elfing; in fact, some lament its creation and prefer it didn't exist.

When it comes to elves, like with everything else, to each his own. The last thing any mom needs is more pressure. If the thought of elf season makes you smile, consider joining the fun. If the idea makes you cringe, pass on it the way I pass on cookie exchanges, caroling and gingerbread-house making.

But, for those who elf, do the non-elf mamas a solid and teach your kids that just like the rest of the year, families all have their own ways of doing things.

And now, for Finn's first trick of the season, he'll trash my bedroom as we play hide-and-seek in our trunk of Christmas decorations.

For more ideas about how to have a little holiday fun with your family's elf, find me on Facebook at Nathalie's Notes. For the rest of you, whether or not you elf, Merry Christmas!

A resolve of one's own

JAN 3

Somewhere between the whirlwind of the holidays and adjusting to the fact that an entirely new year is upon us, there is an opportunity to create a subtle but significant shift in each of our lives. That opportunity lies in looking at the tradition of making New Year's resolutions with fresh eyes.

For so many of us, those resolutions have become a revolving list of failed attempts to do the same old thing, the same old way.

Before I launch into my attempt to convince you this tradition can create meaningful, positive change, I'll share something written by Annie Dillard. It serves as my inspiration to collect the moments of my days in words scrawled in the margins of my notebooks in order to savor them later.

Dillard wrote, "How we spend our days is, of course, how we spend our lives." I think she's right about that, as days quickly turn into weeks, months, years and decades—if we're lucky.

The trifecta of making, keeping and reflecting on annual resolutions is one way I've learned to be a better steward of my days and thereby, hopefully, my life.

And by "keeping," I don't actually mean making good on everything on the list. I mean recording them somewhere to look at later.

As meaningful as creating the list of intentions is, the tradition of reflecting back on them 365 days, and 30 years, later is more so. I've been doing this for decades and treasure the hand-written record of how I have, and haven't, changed over the years.

I've adjusted some things along the way to make this a joyful process instead of just a commemorative guilt trip.

First of all, it helps to remember our purpose on the planet isn't to do what other people say we are supposed to do; it is to pay attention to what we feel called to do. Getting quiet enough to figure out what that is might be a good place to start.

How do you know which resolutions are really right for you? When you write it down do you feel like this is something you should do or do you feel excited thinking about it?

Both of those things can be true, of course, but the pull to lean into something is what motivates you to make it happen. Look at your list of things you want to commit to doing this year. Is it possible you're overreaching? Think of how fast this last year went. Perhaps consider dialing a few things back and maybe leave saving the whole earth for next year.

This isn't a "to do" list as much as it is a gauge by which to check your progress periodically to make sure you're spending time, thoughts and energy on what truly matters to you.

Next, goals work better when you're specific. Pulling from the classic book of resolutions: "losing weight" is less effective than, say, "be able to zip up my winter coat this time next year." Which, by the way, worked for me this year. Plus, I was warmer.

For years, getting out of debt was on my list. And yet, we kept digging ourselves deeper into it, $30 at a time, by not fortifying our resolve with an action plan.

Last year, we finally adopted an ambitious plan. And this year, for the first time since college, I don't have dealing with credit card debt on my list.

It feels pretty awesome. But it took plenty of sacrificing at the Hardy household.

That brings me to my next tip.

After you identify a few top priorities you want to pursue this year, be willing to let the rest take a back seat. For instance, I had "read more" on my list from last year, setting my sights on 13 books.

In fact, I read exactly one book actually written for an adult audience. The rest don't count, because they had Teenage Mutant Ninja Turtles, Lightning McQueen and Elmo as their main characters.

Also, every year since I was 9, I've had "finish writing my book" on the list. Every year, I get just a little closer to that goal—except that I keep starting new ones.

Imagine the library I'll have when I make it a resolution to "finish what I've started."

Don't be afraid to make resolutions you might not be able to keep. Life happens.

If it keeps showing up on your list, and eventually rises to the top, you'll find a way to follow through.

In the movie "Star Wars," Yoda famously said, "Do or do not. There is no try."

Note, the pointy-eared Jedi did not say, "Get it right perfectly the first time or don't bother starting."

Be willing to step up to bat and take a swing. Let yourself be a beginner. You might surprise yourself and get a few resolutions crossed off your list once and for all.

So what does this topic have to do with raising my own Hardy boys?

Being grounded in all the parts of me is essential to making me whole as a mother. It's easy to lose my balance between being the mom I want to be and the me I used to be.

Writing down my resolutions, which range from personal goals to parenting ones, this process highlights where I'm successful as well as identifying my weak spots. This tradition keeps me on the right track, or at least provides a map for when I get derailed.

Still not down with resolutions? Try writing a personal manifesto. If that smacks of a Language Arts assignment you'd just as soon skip, how about simply choosing a personal mantra for the year?

Still not sure you want to spend a few moments thinking about what you want to make happen this year?

Let me close with this question posed by Mary Oliver in her poem "The Summer Day:"

"Tell me, what is it you plan to do with your one wild and precious life?"

Where is the Love?

FEB 4

The mere thought of Valentine's Day has me seeing red. I'm wondering really, where is the love?

Valentine's Day has never been a favorite holiday of mine, and not just because a boyfriend broke up with me Valentine's Day 1996. I'm totally over that. My issue with this so-called holiday is much more current.

For one thing, I'm simply not a fan of the whole candy overload thing. For another, I have kids with allergies and sensitivities to red dye. For all these reasons, this saccharin mid-February affair is the worst of the so-called holidays for me.

Then there's the fact that celebrating Valentine's Day at school has gotten completely out of control.

Those of you who don't have tykes of school age may not think it's such a big deal. After all, in grade school, isn't Valentine's Day about adorable handmade cards tucked into a mailbox fashioned out of paper plates, a stapler and some yarn?

Not any more it's not. Today's Cupid is a little more high-maintenance and aggressively homemade.

My first exposure to this modern Valentine's Day came as a grade school secretary. I saw there that some of the most over-the-top public displays of affection came from parents bearing balloon bouquets, giant teddy bears and bouquets.

They were delivered to class. And the deliveries continued all day long.

It was so crazy one year the bus barn called to say there was no way the buses were going anywhere with all the balloons blocking the drivers' visibility.

Several years later, I learned public gestures of love were no longer enough. These days, it's all about handmade goodies.

The thing is, that means handmade by Mom.

I learned the hard way when Sam came home from pre-school one Valentine's Day with a bucket of clever, creative homemade things, like heart-shaped crayons.

I saved all our broken crayons over the ensuing year, thinking I could do that, too. I also saved a bin of toilet paper tubes, which could be painted and turned into owls or some such.

In reality, that will never happen.

So there we were on Valentine's Eve last year, not packaging our homemade craft, but struggling just to get (expletive) Valentine's cards churned out for 45 little friends. And it soon featured me angrily raising my voice as I tried to get the boys to help.

There wasn't a lick of love in those tiny cards, which came complete with tattoos. No love at all -- not from the boys, who were busy playing while I signed their names, and certainly not from me, who was wondering just what was driving me to do this.

I doubt any of the aforementioned 45 kids cared whether they got yet another Lightning McQueen card, complete with tattoos.

Maybe Sam and Jake would care if they didn't have anything to bring to the table, when the other kids did. But if that really mattered to them, shouldn't they be more invested in the process? Shouldn't they at least be willing to scribble their own names?

As I stuffed the 45 tiny envelopes, I fantasized about rushing to Fred Meyer just before closing time to buy poster board, because "we" had a science fair project due the next day.

That's not ever going to be me, I promised myself. But to make sure I could keep my word, I had to re-think this part of my self-professed holiday mom self.

This year, I mentioned to the boys that Valentine's Day was just around the corner, and if we were going to do something, we should get on it.

The boys decided they want to make their own Valentine's Day cards. And they didn't get that idea from my Holiday Mom/Valentine's Day Pinterest board, either.

For those of you who find joy in getting all clever and crafty, who are able to resist making the kids feel bad for breathing while you're hand-carving their portraits out of chocolate, I bear you no ill will. In fact, truth be known, I'm a little jealous.

But I'm willing to live in my reality, which right now means I let the kids handle the valentines themselves and leave the elaborate ideas to Pinterest. They can be completed in another lifetime in my alternate reality.

If you have it in you, knock yourself out knitting heart-shaped hats for the whole class. Go for it.

I know my willingness to sweep up glitter for the next millennium doesn't get me the same kind of Holiday Mom street cred, but I can live with that. Because as I looked at the prototype card Sam was so earnest in crafting, it struck me as so ... well, homemade. It was sweeter than anything that comes in a wrapper at the store.

Looking at him have at it, I couldn't help but think, there's no way that little boy is going to grow up to be the kind of guy who dumps his girlfriend on Valentine's Day. Not that I'm still pining about that, of course.

When living the dream
is no longer reality

MAR 14

It's with mixed feelings I write this column, announcing another life change for the Hardy family. I'm throwing in the towel on this whole reporter-mama business.

Don't get me wrong. Being a fulltime reporter on the county beat, while raising two little dudes, can be done. Just not by me.

My husband and I worked over our budget. Bottom line, it's just not penciling out for me to keep working, whether I want to or not.

It's no secret: Journalism is a field you enter because you love the work more than the money.

Plus, if you haven't priced daycare lately, for two full-day kids, it rivals a mortgage payment.

Who can argue with that, though? If I can't be with them during the day, I want the best in the business keeping my boys' minds busy and hearts happy. We were lucky to have that with our providers, Creative Kidz.

Then there are associated costs that can't be measured. For me, one of those was being out of alignment with my core values.

In addition to dreaming about being a reporter, I always pictured myself as the kind of mom who was home after school. I imagined being able to walk my kids home, stopping to point things out along the way as we debriefed about the day.

With my job, my boss is as flexible as possible. But that flexibility is a two-way street.

I am often up way too late, or way too early, juggling calls and interviews while packing sandwiches and throwing the boys treats' down the stairs or over the backseat in the car to keep them quiet. And all for just one, more, minute!

After nearly two years of doing my best at both, it turns out I'm not doing either one well enough to meet my own standards. So it came time to make a choice.

Going over the budget made it an easier call. Still, it's hard to realize what you thought you wanted maybe wasn't the best fit in the end.

A friend recently expressed disappointment in my decision. Not everyone gets what they want, she pointed out. And feminists before us fought so we didn't have to choose between career and family.

To her first point, I say: Life doesn't always turn out the way you pictured it, but that doesn't mean you stop trying to create the life you want. To the second, I say: Feminists fought for a woman's right to chose, despite the consequences of disappointing someone.

And that's what I am doing. I am choosing to come back home to be with my boys. I plan to meet my goal of being home with them as long as I can while meeting my goal of publishing a book or two.

I recognize the first will delay the latter, but recently I realized neither will happen as long as I keep trying to maintain balance at the expense of my health and sanity.

I found an exception to George Eliot's saying, "It's never too late to be what you might have been."

My boys are only going to be this age once. If I want to be a stay-at-home mom, writing in the margins, the time for that is now.

Life requires hard choices, and my decision to leave this post to be home with my boys was not made lightly.

Not quite two years ago, I embraced an opportunity to return to the newsroom, a place I loved, to work with people I adore in a job I'd dreamed of having since I was 10 years old.

Then came that awkward moment when my dream job morphed into more of a nightmare, as I tried to balance it with my new reality with two kids, no family nearby and a husband with an equally demanding but significantly higher paying job.

I reached my breaking point on a recent snow day, one of approximately five my kids figure to have in their lifetime. Some friends stopped by as I was trying to work on a breaking story with two cagey kids in the house.

Stories will always break on snow days. It's the nature of the job.

As much as I wanted to be able to celebrate surprise snow days with my kids, I knew my boss also needed stories done well and on time.

I realized in that moment that I too often felt my biggest blessings were a burden. I had lost the little bit of balance I had left.

"But I always wanted to be a reporter," I whined. I was crying, the kind where there's snot and tears.

"So, you're literally living the dream, huh?" my friend said.

Well, when you put it like that, I guess I was. And it it was as clear as the ice on the eaves that my dreams had changed with the reality.

While I've loved most of my time back in the newsroom, I'm at peace with my decision.

I make no guarantees, though, that the aforementioned towels are going to be fluffed and folded once I resume my stay-at-home mom status.

After all, I will have to leave some margins open for writing this column, which will continue running, in addition to keeping up on my long-neglected blog at www.nathaliesnotes.com and embarking on a book project.

Picturing the message

MAR 21

If, as the saying goes, your walls could talk, what would they say about you?

I considered this recently as I looked around my home, scanning for what messages the walls might convey to visitors, and, perhaps more importantly, to those of us who live here.

For one thing, our walls say we value the work of the prolific little artists in our household—not quite enough to frame it, but enough to display on a large board made of wine corks glued into an upcycled window frame. I think the display vehicle says we're kind of crafty as well.

The rest of the stuff on our walls indicate we rarely sit still for a portrait, we most value baby pictures of the boys and we need to find a better solution for dealing with the piles of artwork mined from backpacks, as they collect on all horizontal surfaces.

The truth is, a quick glance around suggests we're kind of lazy about stuff like that. It's an idea further supported by the fact that framed pictures on the wall hang on nails left by the previous owner—when, in fact, they're hung up at all.

While some framed photographs lean against whatever's beside them on a shelf, the majority of my pictures find a home in piles nestled in shoeboxes or in unnamed, unsorted files on my computer.

But don't worry, I took an online class on picture organization. Yes, I did. For real.

I took an entire class about how to organize all those pictures collected over decades, as well as the digital mess I've created since it became possible to take 37 pictures of dinner, or whatever. Called Library of Memories, it was created by Stacy Julian, one of my favorite creative people.

She had me at "library" and "memories," two of my favorite things. And her class changed how I looked at storing my pictures.

I used to be super attached to chronological order. But I've come to understand how little chronology actually matters in the big picture.

When you discover a photograph of someone you love, and it triggers a long-forgotten detail, the last thing that matters is whether it was taken on a Tuesday, or on March 18.

Odds are, if the date is significant, you'll remember it when you see the picture. Otherwise, who really cares?

Instead of chronology, Julian's system for storing and sorting pictures is based on categories and themes.

So, for instance, in an "All about Family" drawer, I have a section for "brothers." In there, I put all the pictures of my boys together.

These are the shots I absolutely love, which are not to be confused with all the pictures I've taken. I've also tucked a few pictures of my husband and his brother in there, as well as some of me with mine. Someday, those might make a great collage or photo album of their own.

I've used this system to pull fun candid shots out of boxes and into frames. Prior to this shift in thinking, I was famous for hanging up pictures with the store-bought family still smiling at us.

The reason the store-bought family stayed on display as long as they did is that I wanted the exact right picture in a frame, put in the exact right place. Frankly, I once considered hanging a picture on the wall a rather permanent act.

As I've become more flexible, I've adopted a new approach for living with our pictures. I've resolved to be blessed rather than burdened by them.

I can make a case for walls talking to us, or at the very least sending a message about what matters to us. So, I want mine to whisper memories of good times gone by and to signal a reminder of what I cherish most: my people in all their messy glory.

If you look around your own walls and realize perhaps they aren't reflecting what you value, here are some ideas that might get them back on message:

Use your words: Turn a favorite quote, lyrics or even a transcript of your wedding vows into wall art by typing them up and then enlarging them. Frame them. And just like that you have a reminder of what matters more than who took the garbage out last, or ever.

Lean in to your commitment issues: For those who share my inclination to lean picture frames against the wall rather than commit to a nail in the wall, consider installing a picture ledge or two so you can tweak your arrangements as desired.

Picture the good times: What better way to tell someone you're glad they were born than to memorialize it with a clock stopped at the very time they arrived flanked by photographs of the day they were born and a current mug of them. I saw a version of that idea on Pinterest and am looking for one more funky clock to help me pull that off.

Think outside the frame: Stretching favorite scraps of fabric onto foam board, or even thick cardboard, and mounting that on the wall is another way to put some personality on display and incorporate hobbies into decor. For instance, I am trying to figure out the best way to do this but I would love to mount a border of Lego plates in the boys' room.

Change with the seasons: Capture the changing seasons from years past in a rotating digital display. For Christmas I received the one thing I asked for, a digital picture frame. It is still sitting on the shelf, showing off some lovely sample images of yes, strangers enjoying places we've never been. But what I have in mind, and will pull off one of these days, is a rotating seasonal slide show. So, say in December, I'll upload pictures of Christmases past to share with whoever is hanging out in the living room.

Oh, and for those pint-sized Picassos, I've got a new strategy: I display current work, then I scan favorites or take pictures of bulky projects and use them as stationery for letters to grandparents, or I recycle them. I'm planning to make a photo book for the boys for Christmas featuring their own artwork.

I like to think I'm quite on top of things by already planning for Christmas nine months away, but the truth is these were on my list of things to do last December, too.

Oh, well, like all good memories, these ideas will keep. If not this year, then next. Heck, even if these ideas don't manifest into reality for years, think of the thoughtful graduation gifts they'll make when my boys go off into the world. Which I understand will happen whether or not I update the portraits on the wall.

Let their gut be their guide

APR 4

Last month, I was surprised to realize it was time to talk with my kindergartner about child abuse, specifically how to avoid it.

I know this is a sensitive, difficult subject. But I believe it's one we must talk about—out loud and often.

But I didn't have enough time to prepare.

Prepare who, my husband wondered when I told him how I felt.

Well, me, of course. Because truthfully, I was more comfortable talking to other people about the (insert the worst adjective ever here) reality of child abuse than I was imagining a day when my son would need to hear candidly that bad things not only happen, but they can happen to him.

I've lost sleep with worries of what could happen to him. But I didn't want him losing any over it.

After looking over some program material for a prevention program a local nonprofit shares at area schools, and giving it some thought, I understand now that the truth is, he will lose less sleep if he is confident he can handle situations as they present themselves. And frankly, I will too.

If you asked him what he should do in the event of a fire, he'd say, "stop, drop and roll" and "call 9-1-1."

But if he was on the first floor when a fire broke out at home, he would tell you he'd get out of the house and head for a neighboring house. That's because we have discussed a variety of what-if scenarios in a calm way, talking through different circumstances.

So I decided to follow up on the presentation at school with a little bit of the same. I gave him some scenarios and asked what he thought he could do to stay safe.

"If someone wants to give you a ride, would you get in?" He shook his head.

"But what if they're super nice and offer you candy?"

"Well, no, I still wouldn't, because it might have red dye in it." Okay, that's not quite what I expected.

"What if they tell you I'm hurt and you have to go with them?"

"Why would a stranger come for me?" Perfect!

"What if they had a Lego Ninjago set for you?"

Sam paused before answering, "Well, that's a tough one, Mama. Because I am trying to add to my collection, you know."

Clearly, some more discussion followed.

You never know what a kid is thinking until you have a conversation like this. So I would encourage anyone who has a kid they love to have a similar one, and sooner rather than later.

Eventually, as I danced around the main point, his dad blurted it out: "Look, buddy, there are some adults who hurt children. On purpose."

It was heartbreaking to watch my 6-year-old process that reality. We sat at the table quietly as it sank in.

"So who are those people?"

"That's the problem," I said. "You can't tell by looking. We have to use other clues to figure it out."

Then we talked some about intuition and what it means to let your gut be your guide.

I think children come into the world with keen intuition, and that survival tool is actually scrubbed away over time by mostly well-meaning adults.

So by the time we are adults, many of us ignore little signs of danger, then big, waving red flags, until it's too late. As a consequence, we get incidents like the one occurring on New Year's Eve in Sheridan, where a 4-year-old was beaten nearly to death, allegedly by his mother's boyfriend.

According to police reports, the boy started biting his nails and wetting his bed shortly after his mother moved in with her boyfriend—a police officer, no less. The mother told police bruises started showing up, as well, and her boyfriend refused to let her bathe the child. Her child.

Education and awareness are the key to abuse prevention. After all, you have to learn the signs of abuse before you can look for them and flag them.

Plenty of kids bite their nails and wet their beds for reasons having nothing to do with abuse. However, I'd bet my life the sudden onset of both in this boy's case were signs he'd come under danger, long before the more obvious ones were missed or dismissed, whichever the case may be.

If that little boy could talk, what would he say? Would anyone listen?

I ask because in 2012, an estimated 686,000 children were victims of abuse and neglect in this country, and 1,640 of them died from it, according to the National Children's Alliance.

We need to be listening. We need to be talking about this, even when we'd prefer to pretend it can't happen to the kids we love.

And one more thing, please. For the love of all that is holy, let's stop silencing our children's intuition in the name of good manners and convenience.

For the most part, I tend to let people be when they interact with my kids. I think it's good for the boys to know the meaning of, "It takes all kinds."

However, when someone uses shaming language on them, or uses language designed to override what I know to be my child's intuition, I step in.

Yes, it can be awkward. But I don't care, because I'm the mom.

Common interactions include others authoritatively instructing them to "be nice." My kids don't have to be nice. They have to be polite, but not necessarily nice. If they don't trust someone, for whatever reason, I expect them to project that.

Also, I cringe at forced affection of the kind, "Give uncle so-and-so a hug."

Early on in this kind of familiar social setting, we adults unintentionally start sending messages validating, or overriding, a child's innate sense of safety.

The most obvious way I see it happening is the forced affection. My view is, if the kid's not feeling it, don't force it.

The other adult will either understand or be offended. Either way, it's his or her problem. My job, as a parent, is to protect my kid's right to set physical boundaries with people.

As most of us know, children are more likely to be abused by someone they know than a perfect stranger. They need to learn early and be reminded often that a parent will back them up, and it's OK to say no.

I tend to use the, "OK, we're leaving. Let's give uncle so-and-so a hug or high-five."

This gives the boys a choice and falls within my manners threshold.

I know this is going to freak some people out, so to be clear:

I'm not saying that if a child doesn't feel like giving auntie a kiss there's some sort of problem afoot. It could just be that the child is in a bad mood.

Perhaps the kid is holding a grudge because of an earlier denied cookie. Who knows?

My point is simply that we don't always have to know why a kid isn't comfortable with something. We just have to let them learn to process those feelings without forcing them to accept ours.

A final word on the forced affection issue:

If you've ever been on the painfully awkward end of watching a parent try to force a child to hug you, it pretty much sucks. Could we just all agree not to do that anymore?

Beware the unintended message

For better of for worse, the little ones are watching us. And if my two kids are any example, they are taking mental notes and making connections from them.

I was surprised recently when my kindergartner came home from school with a library book from the National Geographic Kids series called "Human Footprint." It was written by Ellen Kirk.

On the cover, this book, published in 2010, promises to highlight "everything you will eat, use, wear, buy and throw out in your lifetime." Except, as we quickly discovered, not really.

Sam said he chose the book because he wanted to know "why the landfill is such a big deal."

I wasn't kidding about them paying close attention.

Every night at dinner, we discuss our day. That often that includes stories I'm working on, and a local landfill expansion bid often makes the list. I've accumulated an ironically insane amount of paper dedicated to coverage of the landfill.

Sam evidently recollects how often I've been working on a landfill story, or reading up on issues related to the landfill. So we curled up together to take a closer look at the "Human Footprint."

With its colorful images and kid-friendly infographics, it's a great conversation starter. But the one that ensued in my house was unexpected for me, and probably would have been equally surprising for the author.

Right off the bat, we got: "Your human footprint is the mark you make on the Earth." OK, I get it.

Then: "You're only one person in a country (the United States) that has 308 million people on a planet (Earth) that has 6 billion, 8 hundred million people." Those figures did not appear to compute, but Sam's little eyes grew wide.

And finally: "So with all those people, could your small human footprint really make a difference? Yes. You matter. What you do adds up." Ah! Yes! Reinforcement of a message I preach all the time.

Then things went a little off the rails—for me anyway—with this nugget: "In your lifetime, you'll munch through 12 shopping carts full of candy bars. Yum!"

Um. Say what?

This little factoid got Sam's attention for sure. And with the illustration of shopping carts piled with candy his eyes reflected his take on this mind-blowing statistic.

"So, you mean I'm going to get to start eating that much candy when you're not around to stop me?" Thank you, National Geographic.

With carefully placed emphasis I read further:

"You will eat 14,518 candy bars. ... The sugar from all those candy bars totals 1,055 pounds. That is the same as 211 5-pound bags of sugar. And, it's the reason we have an obesity epidemic in our country and so much illness that is directly linked to our eating habits."

I started to turn the page, but Sam put his hand over mine.

"Mama? Does it really say that last part?"

I paused and eyed the two happy, healthy looking children in the picture.

"No, it doesn't say that, that's just supplemental information for you. Here's a little tip on this page, 'Make candy wrapper jewelry! Since wrappers are made out of different plastics, it isn't easy to recycle them.'"

"Oh! Mama! I'm going to start using my own money to buy candy bars to make candy bracelets. Then I will sell them and use the money to buy Legos!"

By this point, I started drafting a letter to the author in my mind. But to be fair, I've long felt Sam had an uncanny way of taking the most obscure, unintended take-home message from a story.

Moving on, we came to: "In your lifetime, you will drink an astounding 43,371 cans of soda. ... Each day, 178 million cans of soda are popped open across the country. That's more than 2,000 cans per second. ... Recycle your cans. In some states, stores give you your deposit back if you return them."

I was speechless, but not Sam. He piped up, "So, if I start drinking soda, I can earn even more money?"

I said we could collect other people's cans, but no, we wouldn't be bringing soda pop home.

We also popped holes in the assertion that in his lifetime he used 3,796 diapers. That's because he pointed out we used cloth diapers a lot of the time.

By the end of the book, I was a little less freaked out. After all, it's not National Geographic's fault my kid takes a unique approach to things. Nor is it a bad thing to have this information as a conversation starter.

What is "average," anyway? Can we do better?

In some areas, we certainly did better than average. But no, we were no better than most when it came to how much water we used and how much packaging our food comes in.

In fact, the book convinced us to see if we could reduce grocery store packaging by half by doing things like making our own bread. That's because we learned that in his lifetime, he will eat 4,376 loaves of bread.

The book concludes by saying that now that a typical human footprint has been laid out, there are ways to shrink it.

Ultimately, I decided to scrap the letter I was drafting, when I read the author's pitch for kids to eat more vegetables.

She told us, "It takes only 6 gallons of water to grow a serving of lettuce. Compare that to the 2,600 gallons it takes to produce a serving of steak."

So, while my parents invoked images of starving children in other countries, I might just encourage the boys to eat their salad, for the Earth.

National Geographic has expanded this book to an interactive website where you can enter how many cans of soda you drink, or showers you take, and get your own customized lifetime statistics.

To learn more, visit www.channel.nationalgeographic.com/channel/human-footprint/consumption-interactive.html.

Postcards from home

MAY 9

I'm fielding a lot of questions these days about how things are going for my stay-at-home mom redux.

It's a fair question. I usually come back with something flippant about missing bathroom doors that lock and luxuries like uninterrupted conversations and driving in the car with the radio turned up. Oh, and my co-workers, I miss them a lot. Not that my 4- and 6-year-olds aren't super conversationalists, but it's not quite the same.

So, truth be told, three weeks into this transition, I'm still figuring out the answer to how it's going, except to say: We are still adjusting. Some things are awesome, but others, not so much.

Shortly after I left my job, I got a package in the mail with a coffee cup and a note from a friend saying she "missed my mug."

My husband eyed the gift suspiciously. That's because the mug was inscribed, "World's Okayest Mom."

You see, not just anyone can give a gift like that. But it came from the right person. I love it because it reminds me that being a good mom is all relative, so to speak.

Bottom line, we are really doing just fine, even if the contents of my desk are still in the living room, and I haven't even started any of the sewing projects I planned to do once I was back home.

First, there's the fact that I don't sew. Then there's the troubling reality that I don't have the time I thought I would.

In my head, I figured the boys were two years older than the last time I was home, so there wouldn't be any diapers to wash, they would be able to get a drink of water for themselves and I wouldn't have to watch them every single second to keep them from choking or sticking something into a socket.

Alas, it turns out they are also two years more clever. Though they prefer I don't watch them so closely, I probably should.

Also, there's a lot of blood that comes with doing tricks on bikes and playing with sticks. Yes, they can get their own water and snacks, but it's amazing how messy independence can be.

But I hesitate to complain, because that would be like getting to go on vacation somewhere awesome, then complaining about the view from the room. Except not exactly.

This is more like a staycation, and it doesn't feel very vacation-y – not between the whole not really sitting down much thing and the not having a moment to myself thing.

Also, being a stay-at-home mom is a total misnomer. You guys know that, right? There's actually not a lot of staying home at all. But that's a topic for another column.

Who referred to this as a vacation again? Oh, right. Me. My bad.

Shortly before I went on my final paid vacation as an employed person, I told my editor I would be willing to write a story from Palm Springs while I was visiting my parents there.

"Are you sure? I mean, it's your vacation," she said.

And then, as if I didn't know better, I followed up by saying I would basically be on vacation once I was back home with the boys. It came out wrong, but still there it hung in the air, perhaps the dumbest thing I've ever said.

There was an awkward pause as we let that set in, followed by laughter. "I look forward to hearing more about that vacation," she said.

Okay, so there's not exactly an umbrella in my drink and no time for postcards, but I am mostly loving having more time with my little ninja wannabes. Plus, I do get to read for fun now. Actually, it's really just paragraphs at a time while the boys set up a track and practice their tricks before asking me to "Watch, Mom! Watch! No, with your eyes!"

Fine, fine. I'll watch. I am aware that their childhood has already been a blur, and if I blink, "Look at me, Mom!" will just be an echo in my memory.

In honor of Mother's Day this weekend, I raise my mug to all the other "okay" moms out there, who are keeping things real by maintaining a sense of humor and remembering to count their blessings instead of their burdens.

Also, just as kind of a public service announcement, I would not recommend that awesome mug as a Mother's Day gift from, say, husbands.

You say "bored" like it's a bad thing

MAY 30

At the time of this writing, there are precisely 11 days until we experience our first summer vacation with a grade-schooler.

Sam is already counting down the days, not because he doesn't like school, but because he can't wait, and this is a direct quote, "to use my new skills to have a lemonade stand."

He tells me, "There's going to be a lot of math to count all my money. But first I need some money to buy supplies. Can I match socks or something for money?"

Of course, Sam isn't the only one thinking about summer. I've noticed social media is all aflutter with posts like, "How to beat boredom with these easy, low-cost ideas," which touts ideas that, in fact, don't appear to be either easy or cheap.

You know what's actually easy and cheap? The library. Local parks. The backyard. A picnic.

Kids don't need gourmet sandwiches, right? Anyone who has ever prepared an elaborate spread only to be met with a tearful, "But I wanted peanut butter," knows what I'm talking about.

You know what bugs me the most about all this advice to help parents "beat boredom?"

First, I think it's twisted to tell parents they need to find ways to fill all the moments of a day now unoccupied by school. That's just crazy.

Second, I can assure you that my mom didn't worry about this kind of thing. Not. Ever. This whole movement to keep kids occupied and engaged all the time seems to be a modern "problem," and I'm not a fan.

Third, it's a lie. In truth, boredom is awesome.

There. I said it.

For those treating boredom as something to be cured, I beg to differ. Being bored is a luxury. Being bored is having long stretches of time with nothing to do but think, which leads to creativity.

Nobody in history has ever died of boredom.

Boredom leads to having ideas, both good and not so good ones. Boredom means time to try something new. Time to wonder. Time to stare out the window. Or, to count cracks in the ceiling, or blades of grass.

But to read some of these articles, you'd think parents everywhere should prepare to be doomed if they haven't already scheduled every second of summer.

What am I going to do this summer? Um, laundry, maybe minus sorting socks. Supervising backyard play, from a distance. Like from inside the house, where I will be folding the aforementioned laundry. And going to the park. Also, the library. A lot. I'm also open to visiting most places with air-conditioning.

God help me, the boys seem to want to get into BMX biking, so I'm sure there will be a lot of that in my near future. Also, more stained laundry.

But other than that, we're wide open. And that's by choice, not chance.

I want my kids to have windows of unstructured time because you know what actually "cures" boredom? Imagination.

If well-meaning adults can stay out of the way long enough, without pressing play on a show or offering up a cure before the child has time to think up something on their own, the kids will be fine.

Obviously, I'm not advocating leaving kids to their own devices for hours on end. Some guidance and simple supplies are needed.

But kids can make a lot happen with a whisk and a bowl. Add water and it's "Hello, happiness!"

The best antidote for boredom is a kids' imagination. And like our muscles, imaginations must be used. They must be pushed to their limits to thrive, or they risk atrophy.

Far from being absent in the equation, I see parents as playing a key role in fostering these opportunities by offering suggestions, encouragement and, most importantly, the freedom for kids to exercise their imagination.

It's true, I haven't yet made it through a full summer with a school-aged child. So I may have a big, fat mea culpa for you at the end of the summer.

But right now, I'm thinking more like this: If I start getting bugged about small people being bored, I'll have to start charging a nickel every time I hear it.

That could cut into some of that lemonade profit. Just sayin'.

Of course, looking forward to planned trips and spontaneous adventures is an awesome part of summer, too. But, I tend to have more fun being spontaneous when I, er, plan for it.

So last night over dinner, we made a list of things everyone in the family would like to do this summer. There are a lot of repeats from last summer's list: "county fair," "Tunes on Tuesday" and "camping," among others. But we also decided to check out each park in Newberg at least once this summer.

The list is long. We might not get to everything. But it's fun having that posted where we can see the vision we created together.

I plan to master the grill, or at least stop setting food on fire. I also plan to join the kids in the library's summer reading program. That might be wishful thinking, but that's kind of the point.

Also on that list are "bike rides" and "play in the backyard a lot." Just so you know, those came from the kids.

As we enter this season of squeezing lemons, stubbing toes, sunburning shoulders and stretching long days out before us, I want to remember it's a short season in more ways than one. So, most importantly, I'm planning to soak up as much of it as I can.

Minding my lost and found

If you know anyone who geeks out on home organization the way I do, you've probably heard this lovely saying: "Have nothing in your houses that you do not know to be useful or believe to be beautiful."

While the message is meant to be inspirational, it misses the motivational mark with me, because very little in my house fits exactly that description. Also, I know exactly zero people who live in such, uh, serenity.

What no one mentions is that designer and writer William Morris uttered those words in 1894. That's 120 years ago folks.

While his is a lovely notion, with the advent of places like garages, IKEA and The Container Store, I've been looking for a new organizing mantra. Maybe something as simple as: "I know where this goes, and now I will put it there."

For years, my mantra has been limited to "Careful!" I utter it whenever I hear someone opening the freezer or the hallway closet.

If you have no concept of what I'm talking about, the rest of this is probably not for you. But for those who can relate, I have to share my discovery of the missing link when it comes to all my failed attempts to organize things.

"I thought that was a joke!" my husband said when I called to tell him I had finally conquered the problem.

Naturally, he was disappointed and confused when he came home to see that pretty much everything looked the same. While not waving pom-poms in support, he did start to appreciate my home improvements when he discovered fetching ice was no longer a hazard and it was now possible to retrieve something from the dryer without being stabbed in the back by a broom.

A friend introduced me to David Allen's "Getting Things Done" several months ago. Ironically, I didn't feel I had time to read it then, so I moved it around among my various piles of stuff.

Finally, I picked it up and read the first few pages. Allen had me at Page XIV.

"I'll give you new ways to leverage those basic skills into new plateaus of effectiveness. I want to inspire you to put all this into a new behavior set that will blow your mind," he wrote.

"New plateaus of effectiveness?" I didn't know exactly what he meant by that, but I figured I wanted in.

I told Matt, "You have to read this! It will blow your mind."

And then I followed him around the driveway reading out loud from Page XIV.

It seemed he was skeptical. He responded, "I think I'll watch it blow yours first, OK?"

Fine, be left in my dust, or the bitty bits of my blown brain, whatever. And I plunged back in, armed with a highlighter.

A silly but perfect example of working the system is my sock basket. As a policy, I stopped matching socks several years ago, on the principle that life is too short. If you want matched socks, you'll find clean socks in the basket. Match them yourself.

On occasion, the boys agreed to match a batch at a penny a pair. But most of the time, sock drawers were empty.

This was an irritant to The Others in my home. It was not, however, enough of an irritant to get them to actually take on the task personally.

The other day, my 4-year-old wandered into the bedroom looking for the basket. He said he couldn't find any socks anywhere.

I told him to check his drawer. "Mom!" he responded. "Mind blown!"

Getting ready to go on a bike ride used to take almost as long as the ride itself. Now we are able to roll out the door quickly, because our helmets are always in designated cubbies, along with knee pads, bike locks and water bottles.

It is awesome – at least if you are one of us organizationally challenged types. Otherwise, you are probably wondering, "What makes this worth writing about anyway?"

Yes, the victories seem small. But they are significant to me, because as I implement Allen's strategies, I'm not only gaining external peace from internal order, but I'm also getting precious time back.

Did you know people spend, on average, 55 minutes a day looking for things?

I don't mean hitting up Google for the best restaurant. I mean like finding the phone so you can make the call to place the reservation, or the keys so you can drive over at the appointed time, or the gift certificate you've been saving for just such an occasions.

I struggle to find matching socks, missing permission slips and the seeds from last summer's garden. Actually, I eventually found those seeds, but not until I had already purchased and planted new ones.

What I like best about Allen's system is that it's designed to work in a real life setting. It factors in the messy, moving parts. It doesn't rely on a fantasyland where there are no interruptions or on sponsored shopping sprees at The Container Store.

It might sound complicated at first, so much so that I wondered if I should really be investing the time to read the book. But if I can stop spending 55 minutes a day looking for things, that promises to give me back 335 hours a year.

Wow! What I could do with 13 extra 24-hour days really does blow my mind!

Beyond the bon-bons

JUL 4

It should surprise very few to learn that since I switched from working outside the home full time to stay-at-home momming full time, there's been a little, uh, shall we say, "relationship recalibration" around here.

While we aren't breaking any new ground with the whole "who does what around here" argument, I figured it would be worth dedicating at least one column to this futile fight so the rest of you who might be having it know you are not alone.

Honestly, my first draft was an angry journal entry. I considered not submitting the final version because I don't want to pick on my husband. After all, I love the guy.

But I am committed to reality and honesty. And I believe an authentic column about parenting, running as long as this has without at least some mention of that classic argument, would be neither realistic nor honest.

It turns out, my husband is genuinely baffled about why I don't get more done during the day. Probably more puzzling is the lack of bon-bon containers in the bathroom, fancy nails and spa appointments.

For us, the issue came to a head last weekend when both of us were both trying to get major projects done while our 6- and 4-year-olds entertained themselves in the backyard. But that only worked for about an hour.

I suggested he finish his, then give me some time in the evenings to do mine.

"But you have all day, every day," he said, incredulous. I stared back at him, equally incredulous.

Do I? Because it doesn't feel like that at all.

"You're the boss, you can do whatever you want," he said.

I'd prefer to report that comment was met with silence. Alas, it was not.

His is not an uncommon misunderstanding of what it's like at home with little ones. The truth is, my days actually seem to be run more by the boys' bowel and bladder needs, and cleaning up after said needs, than a list of tasks to be accomplished by day's end.

Oh, I make lists. It's just hard to factor in all the little ways things go sideways.

Water spills. It gets cleaned up. Food spills. Floor gets mopped. Someone cuts foot, leaving trail of blood and dirt on freshly mopped floor. And so it goes.

Or, how about simple things like going to the grocery store.

Do you have any idea how long it takes to get two children through Fred Meyer to buy bananas, bread, spinach and tortillas? Forty five minutes, people.

Why? Well, because they wanted to help, or didn't want to help. Because they never have to go to the bathroom at the same time, but do both need to go at some point. Yes, even though they went at home before we left.

This is a familiar fight, even to me, because it surfaced every so often during round one of my being home with the boys. You'd think we'd have learned. And actually, to some extent, we have.

My husband is learning to keep some of his observations to himself, and conversely to make an effort to notice what I actually do get accomplished.

As for me, I've learned that it doesn't matter so much if everyone doesn't get it. I really don't have to defend myself for being the kind of mom who would rather let the boys play peek-a-boo with squirrels on a very long walk home from school than worry if the floors are clean enough to eat off.

Who eats off the floor, anyway? Besides kids, I mean.

The first time around, I was intent on making sure people knew how hard it was to be home with little ones. I wanted it understood it really is work, no matter how good the cause. So I wound up doing a lot of what sounded like complaining instead of being grateful for the time with them.

When my now 6-year-old was a toddler, I overheard a woman sounding much like I probably did as she lamented all there was to do to care for her children. She made them sound like such a burden, and they were within earshot.

She was likely just venting to a friend. But I realized in that moment that I never wanted to make the boys feel like burdens.

This time around, I'm mindful to avoid giving them the impression they are "work." I am trying to balance that with getting their cooperation on lessening the load around here so there's more time to read, snuggle and play together.

Did you know that to do something fun, crafty and hands-on, like making play-dough, it takes 20 minutes to set up before and 15 to clean up after in return for 30 minutes of actual play time? Call me crazy, but I think it's worth every minute. To the kids, it's pure joy.

So when people ask me what I do all day, exactly, I struggle. I once came up with a detailed list of how my typical day went, but I haven't managed to pull that off again.

Annie Dillard said, "How you spend your days is, of course, how you spend your life."

I hope to spend my days focusing on the magic before the mess and on making the people who matter most to me feel cherished, loved and safe—even if they also happen to be the messiest people I know.

A day in the life

When my boys were 3 and 1, I actually took the time to note what, exactly, I did during a typical day.

Of course, this is just a snapshot, as each day has its own rhythm. But I think it makes the point, probably by the time it reaches noon.

I haven't made the time to do a similar exercise since, and some of the details have changed. But I'm basically still on the same merry-go-round of mess, clean up and repeat. So, for those who asked, here is a sample day in the life of this stay-at-home mom:

Between 5 and 7:30 in the morning: Wake up to sounds of my husband trying to be quiet. Marvel that my children slept through the night and pray for another hour of quiet before the party starts. Write, prep breakfast, put in a load of laundry and empty dishwasher as quietly as possible.

Head back upstairs, where Sam finds me stretching in my room. Work in a little yoga with him before his brother wakes.

Sam is the loudest little yogi ever, so Jake is up before long and hits the ground running. Then he falls, hitting his knee on an unidentified object. I don't know what happened, since I was being so negligent as to pay the bathroom a momentary visit.

7:45 a.m. Bring some first-aid stuff upstairs to deal with the scrape. Sam insists his brother wants a boo-boo pack and hurries downstairs to get it. On the way, he falls, too. So there we are, the three of us on the stairs, two-thirds of us in tears.

I suggest we start the day over. We get dressed and come down for breakfast.

8:05 a.m. Notice the box of Band-Aids is suspiciously empty. Find them stuck all over Sam's door. Scrape them off as he explains he was "just decorating."

8:10 a.m. Notice the Neosporin cap is missing. Spend the next 15 minutes hunting for it before Jake finds it and nearly chokes to death.

Change Jake's diaper, but not quickly enough. In the 12 elapsed seconds, he manages to pee all over his beloved stuffed Zebra. Lucky I have a spare.

8:25 a.m. The water I'd set to boil for our oatmeal has evaporated. I switch my sights to almond butter toast with honey.

8:20-8:30 a.m. Have to manage Sam's meltdown over not being allowed to watch "Bob the Builder."

8:32 a.m. Breakfast on the table. Bags packed the night before await, so we can be on time today.

Except I didn't read Sam's mind, thus "messed up" his toast.

8:33 a.m. Have to manage another meltdown because I cut Sam's toast into rectangles instead of his "favorite shape, triangles." FYI: Yesterday, the request was for rectangles.

Jake, on the other hand, loves toast. He doesn't care about the shape. Either way, he thinks it makes a lovely hat.

8:40 a.m. Eat my toast standing up, while combing almond butter out of Jake's hair.

8:55-9 a.m. Clean up, by which I mean the kids, not the breakfast dishes. On a good day, those get thrown into the sink, and on a bad day, not.

Wrangle kids into shoes and car seats. Catch a whiff of stinky realization that I need to change Jake's diaper.

Stupidly smell his pants to see if he needs new ones. He does.

9 a.m. Load boys up for day care and proceed to lock myself out. Have to break into the house. Contemplate how I will explain to my husband that I still haven't gotten around to making a spare key, all while singing "Wheels on the Bus" all the way.

9:30 a.m. Arrive at day care, breathless after carrying 30-pound Jake from the back-40 while trying to keep up with Sam, who can't wait to play trains. As I sign in, I can't resist bragging a little about actually arriving at the appointed time—9:30. Sadly, I'm informed that I had actually signed up for a 9 a.m. drop-off.

9:45 a.m. Determined to work out—and let's be honest, take a shower all by myself—I head for the gym.

Mission accomplished. Squeeze in workout, shower and some writing time in my remote office, aka the locker room.

A few people have asked me why I go through the trouble of going to the gym, when I could just go for a walk with "one of those kid-pusher things." For those who don't know, that would be a stroller.

I suppose it's possible someone who's never pushed one with two siblings in it wouldn't understand that is an exercise in both patience and futility, but not so much it fitness. That's because you're always having to stop to give someone his bottle back or pick up the blanket that you just ran over and will now have to wash before bedtime.

11 a.m. Pick up the kids and drop by the "Tractor Park" on the way home to supervise a play and sharing practice. Watch in awe as other parents are able to relax and read as their children fling sand into my kids' faces.

11:30 a.m. Bribe the kids back to the car with the promise of lunch and an episode of "Caillou." Yes, even if it's sunny.

People treat use of television as a babysitter like it's a bad thing. I'm more of a "most things in moderation" kind of mom. Ad-lib "Wheels on the Bus" all the way home, in order to include all of the "Sweet Pickles" characters.

Since I'm already over my word count, you'll just have to trust me. The afternoon was a blur of crafty activities, clean up, sharing practice, explaining why it's not OK to tow each other by the neck, hunting down remaining strangulation hazards, trying to keep one kid relatively quiet while the other naps, prepping dinner, bum-wiping, re-wrapping the toilet paper on the roll, Googling contents of Sam's giraffe and ideas for how to fix his tail, doing the laundry. The list goes on.

Flash forward to the chaos of the day fading into dinner negotiations, bathtime fun and subsequent tsunami zone, then stories, songs, bedtime. I SAID BEDTIME!!!

Then I clock out.

Just kidding, of course.

At bedtime, Jake is crying for Zebra. Oh, did I forget to mention that he decided to toss Zebra in as I was filling the tub, soaking it? Remember this morning, when he peed on the other one and I was glad I had a spare?

Oops. Didn't get Zebra No. 1 washed and dried in time.

Motherhood is full of dilemmas. Do I give him the zebra that's soaking wet or the one reeking of pee?

I'll leave you on that note.

I know there are many things I missed. I'm sure you can help me fill in the blanks. Hopefully, this is enough to demonstrate what a mad-awesome gig this is.

Think before you toss

JUL 22

Let's be honest. For most of us, saving the whole planet is just a titch overwhelming to contemplate. Yet, anyone who has been paying the least bit of attention knows environmental issues are, well, a real issue.

Whether or not we are of like mind on the local landfill, we probably all agree that reducing the amount of garbage we contribute to it is a good idea. But do we run with that good idea, and if so, to what extent?

As long as we're being frank here, part of the challenge of creating a greener community is that we are completely hooked on convenience. So hooked, in fact, that I think we often feel rather entitled to it.

Walk a little farther down the block to throw something away? Nonsense. If the city, or business owners, don't cough up the money to put refuse bins within convenient reach, the ground will do.

This sounds ludicrous, but look around next time you take a walk somewhere.

People seem to feel entitled to eat and drink at all times, using disposable cups, cutlery and wrappers, of course. And they seem reluctant to be so inconvenienced as to have to wait to throw it away. According to the Environmental Protection Agency, about 30 percent of waste in this country consists of packaging—wrappers, bags, containers and such.

I know changing habits of convenience isn't easy. It is a pain to remember to bring your own bags to the store, your own mug to the coffee counter and to go the extra step to pack a washcloth in a reusable baggie instead of using paper towels.

But it's only a bother at first. Once you get used to it, it becomes as normal as brushing your teeth—with the water turned off, of course.

Before starting this column, I was much more attached to keeping things convenient. Then along came my children.

I wanted to set as good an example for them as I could. Also, I wanted to do my part to make sure there's a little bit of planet left for their children and their children's children.

My first born—Sam, now 6—helped inspire this effort. In the process, doing things that seemed a big bother to me have become just normal operating procedures for him, and by extension, me.

When he recently went on an organized trip, he reported the following to me: "Mom. You have to pack me garbage for lunch. Just garbage."

In response to my confused expression he said, "Not junk food, Mom, just garbage. Like to throw away? Don't send anything recyclable."

I contacted the event organizer to make sure something hadn't been lost in translation. Indeed, this was a large group and plans called for genuinely disposable lunches for the sake of convenience.

You know what? I get that. When you're with a group of excited children, you're basically one stuck zipper away from chaos. That's exactly the kind of situation where convenience is called for.

"This feels weird, right?" Sam said as we packed his lunch.

Casting about for something to put his sandwich in, he hit on the bread bag.

"Wait!" he said. "Put the rest of the bread in the container and I'll pack my sandwich in the bread bag. We would throw that out anyway."

I was eyeing a new, gallon-size plastic freezer bag when he came up with his win-win solution.

Part of what's worked well for me is the way we talk about making greener choices around here. I think there's enough guilt and angst in the world, and enough of it is falling to our children, without putting the entire burden of healing the planet on their little shoulders.

Instead, we try to make it fun to explore outside and foster a connection with the natural world. I think that connection morphs into an affection, which creates a desire to be protective through positive choices.

To me that's an easier message to swallow than some of the scarier ones about how the planet is going to hell and we're doomed unless we all change radically and right now. The only thing we can actually truly change is ourselves, and the example we set to those watching.

Speaking of swallowing things, a Poison Control lady recently asked Sam to identify which of two bottles containing an electric green liquid was poisonous. One was a beverage, the other a cleaner, so I thought the answer was obvious.

Sam surprised both of us when he insisted each bottle was full of poison.

"But which would you swallow?" she persisted.

"Neither, because it's poison," Sam responded.

Uncomprehending, the Poison Control lady looked at me. That was a little bit my fault, I explained. We are label-readers and I have a habit of pointing out chemicals that are bad for you.

"Well, one is a bad nutritional decision, but the other is truly toxic," the Poison Control lady reasoned.

"Actually, they are both toxic," Sam said, holding his ground.

We didn't take the complimentary coloring book, and I walked away wondering if maybe "poison" was kind of an overstatement on my part.

But I like the fact my kids want to know what's in the sunscreen they're applying or the water they're drinking.

We don't always make the most correct environmental decisions, but I love that we're talking about actions and impact, choices and consequences. I hope we always keep that conversation going.

And, of course, that those conversations lay the foundation for action.

Because I said so

AUG 1

Six years. It took six years for me to meet my threshold for accepting unsolicited advice and critiques on my parenting from The Others, which includes family, friends and random strangers.

For those who haven't met them, my boys are 6- and 4-years-old and are absolute angels at all times.

I kid. Besides maybe those keeping them safe there are no angels at the Hardy house, just a pair of awesome, typical boys.

While the first draft of this column was kind of ragey, I decided it would be more helpful instead to issue this public service announcement: People, just because you don't see me discipline my children for misbehaving does not mean it doesn't happen.

If I don't spank my kid right then and there for behaving badly, please don't assume I think the transgression is cute, funny or acceptable. Instead, if you will, please assume that I'm handling it, or that I will handle it shortly. My way. Because I'm the mom.

If it appears that the situation is out of control, which I admit happens when both children seize the opportunity to test me at the same time feel free to offer some kind, non-judgey back up.

Or, even better, help a mama out. This week I had two instances where people helped me drive a lesson home instead of being jerks about the fact that kids are relatively new to the planet and are still figuring it all out.

At the library last week, the boys went to grab a movie. Except when I looked up, they were approaching me with arm loads of them. I was mortified at first that they made more work for someone but quickly realized I needed to make it uncomfortable for them instead of me so they'd learn from it.

I explained the problem, and asked how they wanted to fix it. They apologized to the children's librarian, Ms. Amanda, and then asked her to teach them how to put the movies away properly. She took a few minutes to do that, and they spent the next five fixing their mistake. Parents and children need more Ms. Amandas and less reproachful glaring.

To the chagrin of some, the era of shame-based parenting strategies and spanking kids for the sake of proving you "did something about it" is kind of over. I say "kind of" because there are throwbacks to the old school ways of raising children who insist that all my kids need "is a good spanking." For every single thing they do wrong.

But that "a swat cures all" approach just doesn't factor into my end goal which is to raise kind, thoughtful, creative, confident and resilient children.

I realize that people care about how these younger generations turn out, and because of that I get that family, friends and strangers at Safeway feel they are invested in the outcome of these little ones.

For those reasons I edited my ragey rant into what I hope is a message that translates into a call for grace in how you respond to children in public, and while you're at it extend some grace to those of us making our way as parents whether or children are two days, two years, 12 or 20-years old.

While I welcome stories about what did and didn't work for other people whose kids are older, and I love swapping tips with people who, like me, are still stepping on Legos, I am done with people "should-ing" on me.

So, my dear family, friends and random strangers here's the thing: Thanks for caring enough about my kids to have an opinion. Or, perhaps it's that you care so much about your opinion, but either way, next time you feel like questioning how I'm handling something, my answer for why I'm doing things the way I do them is simple: because I said so.

Find a need and fill it

Suicide has been on my mind a lot lately.

No, not like you might think, but I've been there too.

Following the self-inflicted death of my classmate, Jennifer Huston, then actor and comedian Robin Williams, and most recently Pink Martini percussionist Derek Rieth, my social media feed is blowing up with friends sharing personal stories about depression.

It's depressing reading all of this, a friend observed.

No, it's actually encouraging, I think. And courageous.

In my mind, this adult version of "I'll show you mine if you show me yours" is brave. And also? It's time.

It's time for us to start saying, "See? There are parts of me that are broken, too. I've been there and here's how I came back."

The same thing that worked for me might not work for you, but the more we see that depression and recovery can work in as many different ways as there are people suffering with it, the more possible it becomes for people to feel more OK and less alone in their darkness.

I was going to write about my own battle with clinical depression, but instead I decided to share with you how I found a way to light a candle for Jennifer Huston, instead of just continuing to curse the darkness.

After 12 days of desperate searching by family, friends and complete strangers, Jennifer was found. Tragically it was too late to save her from herself.

I wrestled my way through denial and anger. For days, I was stuck in a loop between those first two stage of grief.

Then I started to pray about what I could do to be helpful instead of feeling so desperately useless. What, if any, silver lining could come of this?

Was there a way to show Jennifer's devastated husband and children that they were not alone? Was there a tangible way to show we cared for them despite, or even more so because of, the sad conclusion of our search efforts?

And God said, actually, yes. Yes, there is. You can fill their pantry with gluten-free and dairy-free food to accommodate their son's food allergies and ease the burden of this transition on them.

But I can't afford to do that, I reminded God.

And He said, "But you can make it happen." And I was like: "Uh, no. I'm not good at that kind of thing. And I don't have the time. Good idea, though."

But God promised people would step in and step up. All I needed to do was be willing to see it through.

You guys!

In the 10 days following my announcement of the Pantry Project, we filled 11 bags and boxes full of gluten- and dairy-free foods, plus a huge box of freezer items and gift cards for local restaurants. We were able to deliver all of that, along with $1,000 in cash for the family to spend as needed. And we did it one dollar and one bag of brown rice noodles at a time.

The platform was a Facebook page created by my friend, Donny Lehmann.

He was inspired to create the Newberg-Dundee Citizen Info Group in honor of three family members murdered in the ultimate act of domestic violence by Randall Engels in 2012. Today, that page has more than 5,700 members, and has bridged our modern social media culture with our old school roots of neighbors looking out for each other.

Through this site, we spread the word quickly. For 10 days, every time I came home, I found a new package of food on my porch. Every time I looked, there were a few dollar bills under the mat or a check in the mail.

This small town's simple mission to feed an entirely different kind of hunger brought people together with a simple purpose, and it gave those of us who wished there was something we could do that something.

The project didn't just help the family, it helped all of us who participated. That's kind of how this business of living in service of one another works, right?

My heart still breaks for Jennifer, and those who loved her, but it is also filled with hope—hope for today, for tomorrow and for what can happen when we show up to say, "Yes, I can help."

Nathan Schrader, owner of the Blue Dolphin Car Wash, summed it up best when he said he wanted Jennifer's husband and their kids to know they weren't forgotten and weren't alone. "Every time they drive by, I hope they remember this community stands beside them," he said.

Schrader and his wife, Crystal, hosted a benefit car wash. Including their own donation, they netted $400. Then their employees, on their own volition, chose to contribute the $200 they had received in tip money.

The rest was collected in dollar bills and checks from people as far away as North Carolina and as close as friends standing in my driveway.

What does all this have to do with a column about parenting? Well, I'm glad you asked.

One concept I'm trying to consciously impart to my boys is the habit of identifying a need and then meeting it.

In other words, don't be the guy standing there with his hands in his pockets. Don't be the guy sitting on the couch asking "What can I do to help?"

Instead, figure it out. Then go do it.

And the best way to teach is by showing, not telling.

As I drove home after delivering everything with a group of friends, I realized what we just pulled off was the epitome of Margaret Mead's eloquent reminder: "Never doubt that a small group of thoughtful, committed citizens can change the world. Indeed, it is the only thing that ever has."

This was a hard column to write. There were so many things I wanted to share but as with all of my columns I pray before, and as I write, and stay open to that still, small voice and this is what came out. I felt there needed to be a story of coming together and showing that there are creative, concrete ways to help each other out. I wanted to help this family but I also I did that pantry project for myself and everyone who wanted so much to do something when there seemed to be nothing to do. I keep the "Find Jennifer Huston" button on my desk to remind me to keep looking. I will never understand what was in her heart and mind that day, but I do know she could've been me. I could've been her. And so I keep looking for opportunities to reach out, to connect and to understand what I can and accept what I can't. It's a long road. But we are, none of us, alone.

Heaven help us

I recently found a new way to be mortified as a mother: I took the boys to church.

They acted like they'd never seen the inside of one before. And to be fair, that wasn't far off the mark.

I embarrassed us first, as we stood in line to register for Vacation Bible School.

"So they stay until noon?" I asked. The nice ladies nodded. "And I just, like, leave?" Again, they nodded.

"Wow!" I blurted out. "If Vacation Bible School doesn't make a believer out of someone, I don't know what would."

I think it may have came off the wrong way, as silence descended as I ushered my confused children into the church.

Once inside, Jake loudly asked, "So, who exactly is Jesus again?"

On the way home that morning, Sam cheerfully told me what he had learned.

"Oh, also, mom. You told me God is all things, right? Well, I said that God is in my boogers and the teacher said, 'No.' So you're wrong about that."

Why, God, why? Why did my child decide to say "boogers" instead of something beautiful and poetic?

Oh, right. This is real life.

In real life, if you decide you want to become part of a church family, you have to jump in somewhere. And it's going to be a little bit awkward at first perhaps.

OK, if you're us, that's a given. But if you're feeling drawn to check out the whole going to church thing, you should understand it is a come as you are kind of endeavor. If you don't feel welcome after a few visits, go somewhere else.

It took me a couple decades to do exactly that. I'd encourage others to get there faster.

Of course, I'm not here to tell people what to do. I'm just sharing what's working in my far-from-perfect life.

In this life, my children manage to get their pants dirty walking the three blocks to church and turn the little, wooden crosses they made inside the church into guns on the front lawn afterward. I thought would be terribly awkward, considering we'd settled on a Friends church, but instead, people were actually quite understanding.

In fact, people have been so awesome, it's made me wish I hadn't missed out on so many years of church. So far, the only thing I don't like is the part about how it's in the morning.

Too often, I experience the incongruous combination of staying up until wee hours watching the debauchery on House of Cards, then rolling out of bed a few hours later for church.

But, despite the morning issue, I love the connections and friendships we're making as well as growing in our faith as a family.

I like knowing that all of my questions are tolerated, even welcomed. And no one acts as if he has all the answers, or as if that's even possible.

Plus, there's been some comic relief.

When we first started going to church, Jake began praying every night, with his stuffed Zebra tucked into his little folded hands.

"Dear God, please turn my zebra into a real one," he'd say. Then he'd open his eyes super fast to see if it happened.

So far, no such luck.

One rainy morning, Jake insisted on wearing sandals so he could be more like Jesus. I pointed out that it was raining.

His older brother countered with the story he heard about Jesus walking on water. I made a note to sign them up for another round of swim lessons, just in case.

On his first day of Sunday school, Sam learned about Job's trials. They are detailed in the Book of Job, once praised by Alfred Lord Tennyson as "the greatest poem of ancient and modern times."

My 6-year-old summarized it this way: "We learned about how God killed all of Job's family and friends. Don't freak out, mom, it's OK. God made him all new ones."

Needless to say, we've had plenty of interesting, clarifying conversations, one of them devoted to reassuring Sam that Job's story didn't break down quite the way he described it.

We also learned from Jake recently that he took us literally when we told him God was always with him.

When asked why he took off from the soccer field to the parking lot by himself, he said he was going to return to the very last place he saw me.

His dad told him we were worried, and that he couldn't go off all by himself like that. He assured us that he wasn't alone because: "Remember? You told me I'm never alone because God is always with me!"

That reminds me that life is full of misunderstandings, and that even though we all get a little lost sometimes, it's encouraging to know there is more than one road leading to home.

I trust each of us will know when we've arrived. We think we do. For our family, gathering at church on Sunday morning feels like coming home.

So what if you don't sew

As I write this, mere days before the ghouls and goblins appear, many moms across America, and a few dads, are sewing Halloween costumes. And I have nothing but applause—even awe—for them.

I am, however, proud to have checked that off my list already. By which I mean, I grabbed two Skylander costumes at Target, right when they went on sale, and told the boys their costume would be a surprise this year.

Then I waited until it was basically too late to do anything about it and planned a big reveal. This elaborate plan included setting the Target bag on the table next to the toast and saying, "Surprise! Open your eyes!"

Costumes, check!

You see, while I would love to be a mom who sews costumes, or anything else, for that matter, I'm not.

I'm a mom who feeds my family fodder for funny stories about, say, the time I made matching pajamas for all four of us. The part about how I sewed the pants shut is particularly hilarious.

In my defense, the pattern I'd picked out for my first big sewing project read like a blueprint for an office building. But I was quite motivated by my husband's doubt that I was going to pull off the pajama project.

"Plaid pajamas for you, my friend," I promised him in response to all the teasing.

"We're going to have matching pajamas?" he said, incredulous.

"Well, more like coordinating," I clarified. "If I go through the trouble of making them, you'll wear them, right?"

"Oh, honey, you bet," he was barely able to contain his amusement.

He was surprised the next morning when I hung the first pair from the doorknob. He was impressed the following morning when I finished the second pair. He looked mildly concerned the third morning, when I handed him his very own plaid pajamas.

It seems I may have been off a bit on the measurements. That evoked the response, "Honey, you made me culottes!"

That wasn't on purpose, honest. I ended up using my seam ripper so much my 4-year-old began calling it "the mistake thing."

The cheerful, Christmassy mantra that got me through the hours I spent with my seam ripper was: "I don't care if I have to staple these (expletive). We are wearing these damn pajamas!"

The finished products reminded me of what one of my best friends calls "aggressively homemade."

They weren't very practical, because I wouldn't let anyone eat or play in them, and no one actually slept in them. The pictures turned out pretty cute, though.

Another time, just as I was due to deliver Jake, I got it in my head I wanted to embroider Christmas stockings for all of us, including our dog. Never mind that I'd never done such a thing.

My husband encouraged me to consider glitter and glue instead of needle and thread, but his suggestion didn't match the picture in my head.

The stockings turned out fine, except that I hated the "M" on Matt's. I have put fixing it on my to do list the last five Decembers.

I should've fixed the sloppy "M" when I first discovered it. But with all the stuff that had to be done before the baby came, Matt said he'd rather live with a "crappy 'M,' and not that I'm saying it's crappy" than a stocking forevermore labeled "att."

Given stories like that, no one at my house is sad or surprised that I don't sew costumes. In fact, members of my family are relieved.

Plus, it leaves me free to consider doing other things, like making a Skylanders pinata for Sam's birthday party.

Notice I said "consider." I thought about it, then caught myself and came down firmly on the "no" side.

Besides, I already had my hands—and counters—full with the extravaganza I was planning for Sam's seventh birthday on October 7. I happen to think being born is kind of a big deal, so we are big on birthdays around here. And "golden" birthdays come around just once, so I was planning to make a fuss.

Here's the catch:

Yes, my kids love it. But that's not exactly why I do it. I actually do it because I love it. I truly do.

But sewing costumes? Not so much.

I have friends who are sewing finishing touches right this moment. They aren't sewing their kids' costumes to show me up, though. They are sewing them because they take joy in it, and that's a critical distinction.

Too often, I think, we project our own insecurities on others. We assume their choices amount to a commentary on ours.

Trust me, they aren't. And if you can embrace that message, you are welcome to send cash to compensate for the therapy expense I saved you.

Because Sam delights in all things holiday, he loved and truly appreciated every detail of his golden birthday, from the seven gold star balloons to the gold star sprinkles on his lunchtime grapes.

I know, I do go a little crazy sometimes. I'm not sure I should tell you, but I wrapped his lunch in gold paper to make it even more fun. Also, did you know they make golden Oreos for just such occasions?

My younger son, Jake, will be a little harder to impress on his golden birthday. He'll be 14 then, and he already tends to keep his joy tucked inside.

I don't think decorating his high school locker in gold foil will cut it. Luckily, I have a few years to reflect on potential alternatives.

In the meantime, I'm considering making a Christmas tree skirt this year. And maybe an advent calendar. Or not.

Special Bonus Chapter:

How to Be a Perfect Parent

{This page intentionally left blank.}

Acknowledgements

My heart is so grateful for the thousand little things that contributed to making this project possible but there are a few people I'd like to thank specifically for helping see this dream through to publication.

My deepest gratitude to:

My family, or course, who can always count on me to have a pen stuck in my ponytail and a scrap of paper nearby. For being patient while I wrote something down "real quick." Thank you Matt, Sam and Jake for dealing with "deadline mommy" when she comes and for embracing that part of me.

To my Mami because everyone should have a mom who believes they can be on Oprah. And for teaching me Feng Shui back when it was just called "cleaning your room." For my childhood, for holding my grudges but also for forgiveness. And for all the other things. So. Many. Things! I had no idea. Aj ja teba.

To my Tati for teaching me attitude is everything. Even when it was annoying. For taking pictures of everything from food to road signs before it was a thing. For my childhood and for laying track to the road I'm on today. For your faith in me. And, for taking notes along the way. And, for being a writer anyway. Aj ja teba.

To Martin, for the judo matches, the secret English spoken in an otherwise Slovak house and for getting my feet used to stepping on Legos.

To my girlfriends, and even a dude or two, all of you. You know why. No words can express how thankful I am for each of you in my life, for your support, encouragement and unconditional love. You are among my most cherished blessings.

To the Bladine family who own and operate a rare, independent newspaper and allowed me to find my voice there. And for paying me to do it.

To Steve who said "yes" to this column, encouraged me in this work and never complained about my affinity for the em dash and even occasionally let me make up words. And, for teaching me to always remember the readers.

To Racheal for her grace on deadlines and in general. And also for suggesting that I do nothing about some things, which blew my mind—who knew that was an option? And also for understanding that deadlines, like Christmas, come as expected and yet always seem to be a surprise.

To Jennifer who saved me from ... myself and who always knew what I meant to say even when I didn't. And for the salted-caramel ice cream on deadline.

To Hilary for my "world's okayest mom" mug. And for getting it. Always.

To Ben, Carl, Don, Jim, Karl, Marcus, Marna, Molly, Nicole, Ossie, Paul, Robert, Starla and everyone else at the *News Register*—you know who you are—who made it a joy to come to work even when the work itself wasn't always such a joy.

The readers of my column and blog.

To Randy and Linda for giving me a chance with Ridenbaugh Press. This is already fun!

To Scott Carl for the last-minute "yes" to bail me out to create designs that actually match the picture in my head, and for being so patient with all of the emails. So many emails.

To Sue Lamb, a kindred boy mama, for the encouragement and editing help.

To my blog readers and Facebook community for your sharing, your ideas and your encouragement.

To Christina Katz, my friend and writing coach for helping me stand on the platform made for me. And, for helping me create it.

To Google, because I don't know how parents did it before you.

To God, who made it so. And to Grace, without which ... none of this.

Nathalie Hardy is a national award-winning columnist and reporter who majored in journalism when she realized she could make a living talking to strangers.

Since becoming a mother she manages to keep writing in the margins as she strives to be more Zen, less banshee. This book is a collection of some of those notes.

Hardy has published freelance articles for numerous local, regional and national publications including Poets & Writers magazine. She facilitates journal writing workshops in person and at Big Picture Classes.com.

Hardy was a nerd before it was cool. She graduated with a journalism degree from Western Washington University in Bellingham.

Talking to strangers, talking about feelings and eavesdropping in public are a few of her favorite things, She even goes so far as to call it working. A writer, she believes, is always on the clock. To pay the bills between writing projects she took field notes from the following jobs: various accounting departments, as a log clerk in a lumber mill, waitress, office secretary and a grade school secretary. And, as a general assignment reporter on the Oregon coast and covering the county government beat for the *Yamhill-Valley News-Register* where she interned in 2000 and started writing her parenting column in 2008.

She served a stint on the Carlton City Council and volunteered at a Women's Crisis Center advocating for women and children to live free of domestic violence. She believes eye contact and connecting with strangers can save us from ourselves.

She lives in Newberg, Oregon with her husband and two sons. She's been keeping it real, since before it was a thing, on her blog, www.nathaliesnotes.com for a decade.

NEED MORE?

Additional copies of this book are available from Ridenbaugh Press.

Visit our web site at www.ridenbaugh.com and the bookstore and catalog available there.

RAISING THE HARDY BOYS

__copy/copies, $15.95 each

Name _____

Address _____

City _____ State _____ Zip _____

Email _____

Ridenbaugh Press
Box 843, Carlton OR 97111.
by phone (503) 852-0010.
by e-mail stapilus@ridenbaugh.com
http://www.ridenbaughpress.com

Made in the USA
San Bernardino, CA
22 December 2014